unbelieve

poems on the journey to becoming a heretic

Marla Taviano

dedication

in grateful memory of
Rachel Held Evans

whose words, love,
brilliance, and humility

changed the entire course
of my life over a decade ago

I owe her a debt
I could never repay

I promise to forever
pay it forward

to you (and me)

if you're asking questions
having doubts

feeling anxious
even scared

I see you
I *am* you

this book is for both of us

RHE

when Rachel died on May 4, 2019
I cried for days—for her family and friends

for all of us who loved her and depend on
her words and will never get any new ones

two years later, something makes me think
of her and my breath catches in my throat

my chest constricts as I realize all over again
that she's gone and never coming back

in the weeks after she died, I re-read all of her
books and I knew what I had to do, I had to

get these thoughts into words on paper
and this book out into the world, I had to

it took me a minute but here she is

humdrum

for 4 years, okay 5, now 6
I try to write a book about

my shifting faith
my unraveling beliefs
my evolving understanding

my blah blah blah blah blah
highlight delete highlight delete

reading my own story
should light me up
not put me to sleep

bless his heart

my dad
wants me to write
a blog post
detailing all of my
theological beliefs and why
I believe them so
I can put an end to
the confusion
and people can stop calling me
a heretic

saturated market

on the one hand you have everyone
and her sister writing books

about their deconstruction but on the other
I have friends who told me just yesterday

Marla, you are the only person
I feel safe talking to about this

so I guess there's room for one more book

long story short

scrapped my wordy drawn-out
deconstruction saga

and swapped it out for
angsty poetry

pile of spaghetti

I like books organized
into sections, categorized

with a clear vision
of logical progression

I tried to do that here but
the neatness felt like a lie

because it was

not happening

a big part of what I've
learned over the past 10

years is how to sit in the
discomfort and tension

of not knowing, of not yet
arriving, of imperfection

but to pretend that I can take

ten years of agonizing, reading,
crying, praying, learning, unlearning,

banging my head against the wall,
cram it into 200 pages and think

you're going to arrive at the
same point I did, just like that?

unthinkable

inspo hits like water drops

I used to think
I thought in
facebook posts
while I was standing
in the shower
but now I realize
they were poems

read between the lines

when everyone
wants you to
explain yourself
poetry
is
an act of
resistance

I was wrong

I spent a whole lot of time for a whole lot of
years making sure I knew it all, got it all right

anything I had to do to avoid that uneasy
and discomfiting feeling of wrongness

I finally opened my mouth and inserted that first
bite of humble pie and yes I gagged and choked

a time or two or six but it started me down
this beautiful path of admitting I was wrong

about not one, two, or six things but a whole hell
of a lot wrong about a whole hell of a lot

couldn't see the poetry for the prose

maybe that should've
been my book title

I know there's not
much new under the sun

but a poem might be
a fresh way to see

an old gem of an idea
in a different light

tip of the iceberg

I'll only scratch the surface of my
glacial-shifting faith in this book

with an occasional deep dive to get
a glimpse of what we're dealing with

but just to warn you—
there's no oxygen down there

you'll have to keep coming up for air

there once was a

very good Christian girl
who had all the answers
it was so very simple
quite quite clear
the Bible made it so

circa 2009 (pre-hashtags)

Hi! Nice to meet you!
I'm Marla,
wife, mom, and
child of the King.
I write books
mostly about marriage
and parenthood
and I speak to groups of
women on a variety of topics
(like sex).
I love to read and write,
take photos of my kids,
hang out with friends,
study the Bible,
and I dream of taking a trip to
Cambodia someday.
I love thrift stores
and antique shops
and yummy food
and my Xanga blog
and libraries.
I'm just really blessed.
Like really
really blessed.

looking back I see it

my writing was so predictable, mass-produced
on a Bible belt in an evangelical jargon factory

like Campbell's Christian-Os heated in a pan
and served in a translucent Tupperware bowl

like canned French green beans and Cream Of
Christian mixed in a Corningware dish

like magenta jellied Christianity Sauce
plopped on a ceramic Christmas tree plate

in a perfect cylindrical shape right
down to the identical uniform ridges

she was on a mission

to wake up a sleeping world
proclaim truth
accept Jesus
or HELL

can you feel the urgency?
he could come in the
clouds any minute

AND THEN IT WILL BE
TOO LATE FOR YOU

a planet at war
Christians on one side
the world on the other
each time a Democrat took office
and let women have abortions
or gay people get married
it felt like we were losing

but we knew better because
not only did our ancient Bible
tell us every single thing we
needed to know
about how to live *today*
it also predicted the end
of the story

we would win
nothing else mattered

someday (maybe soon)
this world would burn
so recycling is pointless and
climate change is who cares?
God would make a new one

and anyone who'd asked
Jesus in their heart
would live in heaven with him
forever and ever and ever

simple
clear
absolute

it all went according to plan
for well over three decades

and then something happened

what happened?

books happened
okay and
a lot of other stuff
but mostly
books
so many
books
so so so sooo many
books

reader beware

"Books can be dangerous.
The best ones should be labeled:
'This could change your life.'"

—**Helen Exley**

to the tune of beer (Coke) bottles

Ninety-nine dangerous books on the shelf!
Ninety-nine dangerous booooooks!
Take one down, burn to the ground,
Ninety-eight dangerous books on the shelf!

Ninety-eight dangerous books on the shelf!
Ninety-eight dangerous booooooooks!

pool trip / guilt trip

summer 2010 / lounge chair / neighborhood pool
book choice remorse / *The Hole In Our Gospel*

pools are for chick lit / not "are you saving the world
hard enough to call yourself a Christian?"

my little girls busy with Pringles and Twizzlers
I stick a vine between my teeth / bite down / chew

author Richard Stearns in Uganda / meets AIDS orphan
in a hut / raising his younger siblings alone

watched their parents die / slow, horrible deaths
their graves lie / just outside the door

Richard wishes he was back / in his safe bubble
before he knew about AIDS orphans / in Uganda

I wish I'd brought *What a Girl Needs* / to the pool
instead of this downer book / reach for Twizzlers

Richard cries / repents / God forgive me for ignoring
the world's suffering and asks / if the gospel is

good news to the poor / what good news have
Christians given the world's / three billion poor

"What gospel have most of us / embraced in the

twenty-first century? / A gospel with a *hole* in it."

I do not like this, Sam I am. / I like the other gospel
where Jesus died for our sins / so we can go to heaven

all we do is ask him into our hearts / not all this extra stuff
just get people saved / their poverty is not my problem

I am so uncomfortable / can't stop reading / can't unsee
feel the earth shift beneath me / can't even finish my Twizzler

irresistible revolution

Shane Claiborne grew up in the Bible belt
a church building on every corner

I can count at least 7 churches
in my tiny hometown (pop: 2000)

he never met a Muslim or a Jew and
was dissuaded from dating a Catholic girl

because she prayed to Mary and
duh, Catholics weren't real Christians

then he spent time in India and
met some poor people in the U.S.

and I spent some time in Cambodia
and met some poor people in the U.S.

and he/I start to feel really uncomfortable
with the Christianity we'd lived for so long

and then he says, "I had come to see that
the great tragedy in the church was not that rich

Christians do not *care* about the poor but
that rich Christians do not *know* the poor"

four-letter words

if you've never lived inside / the bubble of
evangelical Christianity it / might surprise you

to find that l-o-v-e / and p-o-o-r were new
and controversial subjects for me / at age 35

another lifetime

my kiddo was looking through
an old Bible of mine a few years ago

you didn't even underline James 1:27
who even were *you?*

God Loves Everyone

God loves the rich
the same as the poor.
He does not love
one more than the other.
He loves the sister the same
as the brother.
He loves the father
the same as
the mother.

—Marla R. Yoder, age 7 (July 21, 1983)

coming unraveled in monkey town

Rachel Held Evans and I were the
same person as kids teens young adults

super zealous for God and Scripture sword drills
Sunday school regular church Sunday night church

Wednesday night youth group knowing apologetics
like the backs of our hands always ready to give an

airtight defensive answer to anybody's doubts
about Christianity *same person*

I used to be a fundamentalist, she wrote,
"Not the Teletubby-hating, apocalypse-ready,
Jerry Falwell type of fundamentalist, but the kind
who thinks that God is pretty much figured out
already, that he's done telling us anything new.

and that's where our paths diverge because I *was* the

Teletubby-hating (gay agenda!)
apocalypse-ready (*Left Behind* series!)
Jerry Falwell (shook his hand as a kid!)

type of fundamentalist

100%

"Certainty is missing
the point entirely."

—Anne Lamott

growing up evangelical

someday I'll deep dive into my childhood to get
a better sense of how evangelical cult(ure) impacted

my life / as of right now memories are scattered
I haven't yet pieced them together in a cult(ure) quilt

we had sword drills and clown ministry (true story)
vacation bible school where I memorized hundreds

of verses for fake money to spend in a store and
missions conferences where missionaries told tales

and dressed up like people from other countries
sunday school and church every sunday morning

then church on sunday night and wednesday night
youth group, 5th quarter, white water rafting, camp

evangelizing my classmates and my entire public
high school in my valedictorian speech omg

I didn't try alcohol until I was 34 and
I didn't try sex until my wedding night

I was so good and took it all so seriously and have
a crapload of unpacking to do and I'm gonna need

wine and some big girl panties for this field trip

christian supremacy

when your entire identity is built
on being better than other people

it can be unsettling when
you find out you're not

her words changed my life

Marla Taviano / recovering mommy blogger
does online read-alongs / her summer 2012 pick:

Evolving in Monkey Town:
How a Girl Who Knew All the Answers
Learned to Ask the Questions
(by Rachel Held Evans)

she (I) was not ready

from my blog:

I'll be honest.
When I first heard about this book,
I was scared to read it.
I was already feeling tender about
my new views on loving the poor
and seeking/doing justice
and reeling from the fact that I'd
somehow missed this HUGE part of the gospel
my whole Bible-reading life.

The last thing I needed was a memoir
by some good conservative Christian girl
who started questioning stuff she'd
believed in since she was a kid.
Especially a memoir with the words
"evolving" and "monkey" in the title.

I've always considered myself SUPER
grounded in my faith and SUPER
well-versed in absolute truth
(and secretly SUPER scared of
reading/hearing something that might
maybe possibly put the tiniest chink
in my armor of definite certainty).

So I didn't read it for a while.
And then I thought,
"What am I so scared of?"
And I read it.
And it made me s-q-u-i-r-m.

So I tucked it away and forgot it even existed.
I'd read Rachel's blog every once in a while,
but it always made me feel uncomfortable,
so I mostly stayed away.

And then, evolving and monkeys aside,
my own tension and wrestling got more intense.

I plopped myself in the middle of the
Trayvon Martin case (because I realized
my Black friends really cared about it),
and it kick-started an eye-opening
exploration of racial issues in
our country (in the past and n-o-w).

I shook my head at the strong, strong
opinions we Christians have about
what we wear to church and why.

I apologized to Democrats [see Appendix A]
and started feeling super rubbed-the-wrong-way
whenever I got forwarded emails from
Christians spewing venom at the President.

I started re-writing my first published book,
From Blushing Bride to Wedded Wife,
(to release as an ebook) and sat agape
at some of the regurgitated Christianese
and Bible verses I quoted glibly
(and often out of context).

I asked myself if keeping gay folks from
getting married would've been at
the top of Jesus' To-Do List while
millions of people around the globe
are starving and why the heck didn't
he ever mention homosexuality in one
of his Mount Sermons or Temple Sit-Ins
so we could know how to respond to
this issue? Would that have been so hard?

I read some books about women
*(*Half the Sky, Half the Church, *etc),*
and I wondered if God really created us
girls to stand in the background while

37

men do all the important stuff?

And if I'm so stick-to-the-Bible like
I say I am, why did I not think twice
about speaking (teaching? preaching?) to
170 men about s-e-x back in October
(when the Bible says women shouldn't teach men),
and why do I not wear a head covering when I pray,
and why is my father-in-law's hair longer than mine?

Am I picking and choosing (gasp!)
which parts of the Bible to follow??
And then I read a book called
The Blue Parakeet, *and when I was done,*
I picked Monkey Town *back up and*
read it from cover to cover again in about 2 hours.
And holy cow. Holy. Cow.

knock knock

who's there?
older white man
hands full of Bible tracts
and Baptist Church invites.

"Do you know Charles Stanley?
We believe what he believes."

a wee bit ironic/sad/funny
to claim to follow Jesus by way
of an American octogenarian preacher
but I get it

replace [Charles Stanley] with
[your own favorite infallible theologian]

"Do you know Rachel Held Evans?
I believe what she believed."

except Rachel would probably
tell me to think for myself
and then we'd share a knowing giggle

supremacy + ignorance

I was 30-something
when I first realized

Mennonites had been
caring for the poor forever

maiden name Yoder
lived on Mennonite Church Road

sat one street over from
another Mennonite church

in those holier-than-thou
non-denominational pews

thinking Mennonites were
less Christian than we were

non-denominational

what does that even mean? / not sure
might be code for / undercover Baptists

life happens: a timeline

(July 2010) take a missions trip to
Cambodia with our church

(2011) save money to go back
with our girls in December

(Oct. 2011) husband has a massive
heart attack and almost dies

(Dec. 2011) take a five-week trip
come home with plans to move

(Jan. 2012) rush husband to ER
chest pains / heart attack #2?

(2012-2014) panic attack / severe anxiety
lost job / house short sale / deeper in debt

(Dec. 2013) move into Abbey Lane
apartments with refugee neighbors

(2014) one of the hardest most
beautiful years of our lives

(Jan. 2015) move to Cambodia where
we'll live the next five years

dear women in Michigan,

I offer you this apology
over a decade late

remember that time you invited me
to speak at your Christian ladies weekend
retreat called something-something-inner-
and-outer-beauty-in-Christ

and instead of sticking to the script I
blindsided you with soapbox sermons on
human trafficking and poverty in Cambodia?

oops,
Marla

denominations

if the Bible is clear, why are there 200+
Christian denominations in the United States

and 45,000 worldwide all reading the same Bible
but coming to wildly different conclusions?

the pastor conundrum

if all we need is the Bible
and the Bible is clear
what's not clear is why
we'd go to church every Sunday
and listen to a guy
preach a 45-minute sermon
extrapolating Scripture
that's already clear
couldn't we just read the
clear clear words
on our own at home?

monotony

have you ever sat in church
week after week after week

and thought *I've heard this exact sermon*

so
so
so

many times?

aren't you
tired
bored
over it
already?

I only want to watch
reruns if they're
Schitt's Creek

chirp chirp

yellow book, small blue bird
on the cover / *Blue Parakeet*
so far so safe

subtitle: *Rethinking How You Read the Bible*
red flag

voracious Bible student Scot McKnight,
devours commentaries / learns Greek
gets disturbed / starts asking questions

"no one does everything the Bible says"
(*I do!*)

"we all pick and choose"
(*I don't!*)

if we're really doing everything the Bible commands:

why aren't we washing people's feet?
why don't we observe the Sabbath?

why do we give our tithe only to our church,
when the Bible says to give to both the temple and the poor?

heck, why are we not selling our possessions and
giving everything to the poor like Jesus said to do?

why aren't all Christians prophesying, doing
miracles, and speaking in tongues?

why do we think "homosexuality is unnatural" is
absolute truth, but "long hair on a man is unnatural" is fine?

I liked Christianity a whole lot better before
I knew you could ask all these questions

george & the man in the yellow hat

word choice is important / *doubt* raises red flags
curiosity is more acceptable / less threatening

instead of starting from a place of knowing it all
then doubting what I've always known to be true

what if I start from a place of knowing I know just
a little / and want to know what else there is to know

becoming curious about why the Bible says
what it says and why we interpret it the way we do

narrative: *oh, so you're doubting your faith?*
narrative reframed: *nope, just getting curious!*

mar (la/garet)

Judy Blume prolific and
controversial author wrote
an "edgy" book in 1970

Are You There, God?
It's Me, Margaret

I read it in the 1980s
and hid it from my mom

reread it decades later
free as a bird

Margaret is almost 12
moves to a new city and school
navigating life / puberty / boys

Marla is 43
moved to a new country
has three daughters around Margaret's age

Margaret's prayers concern religion indecision
Jewish like Dad or Christian like Mom?
and *God please please please*
make my boobs grow

Marla doesn't know if she
wants to be a Christian anymore

and the big boob prayers
never worked for her so
shrug

we both asked God for a hint but
God just smirked

are you there, God?

it's me, Marla
and I have a lot
of questions

precisely

"If you aren't
questioning the Bible,
I have to wonder
if you're even reading it."

—Rachel Held Evans

the gospel in four easy steps

Step #1 bow your head, close your eyes (no peeking)
Step #2 confess your sins (only 4 years old? you'll think of
something)
Step #3 accept Jesus as your personal Lord and Savior
Step #4 wait for your Get Out of Hell Free card to arrive in the
mail

toddlers going to hell

I asked Jesus in my heart
when I was three years old

THREE YEARS OLD

I used to lie and say four
when I shared my testimony

because four-year-olds are so
much more cognitively-developed

because I didn't think people
would believe the truth

why do we tell tiny people they
have to accept Jesus or burn in hell?

do we actually think they
fully grasp the concept?

dear God please

fear-based prayers
knock-on-wood prayers

traveling-mercies prayers
just-in-case prayers

super-duper-stitious prayers
cover-my-ass prayers

I still find myself
praying these sometimes

I can never remember

is it by grace you're saved
through faith and not by works?

or faith without works is dead?

literal(ish)

it doesn't matter / what you *think*
or what you *feel* / Marla

it only matters / what the Bible *says*

except of course / for the parts
we don't have to / follow anymore

funny

the people who tell me they believe
in a "literal interpretation of the Bible"

are the exact same people who tell me
that any talk of freedom from oppression

in the Bible is "spiritual" or "metaphorical"
and not the slightest bit literal at all

mental gymnastics

it must be so exhausting
to be a biblical literalist
and have to justify
"slaves, obey your masters"
or you could
just be like D
a Christian man
who told me that
if his daughter was abducted
by a sex trafficker
then yes
he'd expect her to
obey her enslaver

what she said

"Stop being
so literal."

—Film and Television's Moira Rose

The Bible Tells Me So

"I believe God wants us to
take the Bible seriously, but
I don't believe he wants us to
suppress our questions about it.
I don't believe he wants us to
be in constant crisis, in a
stress-reduction mode of having
to smooth over mass floods,
talking animals, or genocide."

—Pete Enns

slippery slope

two summers late 90s / camp counselor
ice breaking team building with campers / fun

and sometimes terrifying / steep muddy hill
in the middle of the forest / led into a ravine

trees cleared from the slope / but plenty of
roots and rocks left for / fun

sit on your butt / hold the handle thing
on the rope thing / take a deep breath

ignore the raging fear / let the gleeful
campers give you a shove / so fun

it will beat / the crap / out of you all the
way down / but at the end can you look

back and say you had / fun?

not really

word from wikipedia

a slippery slope argument
in logic
critical thinking
political rhetoric
and case law
is a consequentialist
logical device
in which a party asserts that
a relatively small first step
leads to a chain of
related events
culminating in some
significant effect

it's all downhill from here

if you let two men get married
everyone will want to start marrying

10-year-olds and goats and I think
something about wearing bikinis

escarpment of annihilation

for fundamentalists, RHE said
every single belief is essential

change is not an option and the
world has to stay exactly as it is

or your views—and you—are screwed

"Christianity sits perpetually
on the precipice of doom,
one scientific discovery
or cultural shift or difficult
theological question away
from extinction."

—Rachel Held Evans

like a snowball down a mountain

once you start plucking
scales off your eyes
they tend to keep falling off

once you pull a loose piece of yarn
the whole sweater
really can unravel

once you open the floodgates
it's hard to shove the water
back behind the dam

once that first domino falls
it's almost like there's this
I don't know … *effect*

overheard

whispers
I think she might be…
backsliding

oh hell no
I'm heading down
this puppy
face first

fortunately yes

"The truth may set you free,
but first it will shatter the
safe, sweet way you live."

—Sue Monk Kidd

let's start from the top

the whole slippery slope fallacy / analogy
makes the added assumption that you

started out at the top / in the superior position
but if that were really the case / if I started

at the summit and slid to the bottom
wouldn't it have been easier than it was?

it felt more like an arduous exhausting
climb which leads me to believe I might

have started at the bottom / where you can
only see what's in front of your face

where you can only see what's obvious
where you can only take things literally

where you can't see with the eye of a bird
with no concept of where you are in the world

you think you ARE the world

what happens when you realize you didn't start out
on top of the mountain and slide down into a pit

you started at the base, felt the itch to climb
and see the world for what it really is

and oh my god what a view

not as scary as I thought

there's definitely something
to that slippery slope

but here's the
magic of it all

each new(-to-you) true idea you embrace
and each harmful belief you let go of

gives you just enough bravery
to tackle the next

me neither

"I am not comfortable
in a closed system where
there are no questions left
to ask, or where questions
are shunned as heresy."

—Madeleine L'Engle

hold that thought

it's so hard to write a book when
everything you think and feel keeps

changing, evolving, slipping through
your fingers, hurry hurry write write

before you no longer believe what you
just said or you honestly no longer care

yes and yes and yes

"The only way I have ever understood,
broken free, emerged, healed, forgiven,
flourished, and grown powerful
is by asking the hardest questions
and then living into the answers
through opening up to my own terror
and transmuting it into creativity.
I have gotten nowhere by retreating
into hand-me-down sureties or
resisting the tensions that truth ignited."

—**Sue Monk Kidd**

from a brother in Christ

As far as I can tell,
the principle difference
between you and me
is that I'm drawing
directly from Scripture
instead of some other
book or
opinion or
movement.
And the trouble
with the latter
is that it's often
garbage.

absolutely addled

"She is too fond
of books, and it
has turned her brain."

—Louisa May Alcott

he wasn't finished

Am I bothered that you try to
manipulate people
into thinking
garbage
thoughts
and getting fixated on
garbage
distractions?
Very much so.
I absolutely should be.
My letter was specifically addressing this
garbage.
But the problem
you have with the former
is that you believe we can't know
what the Bible means.
Again, this is you taking an
unbiblical stand in favor
of your own intellect or
experience or teaching
that you have learned from
other books
and movements.
And so you fill your mind with
garbage
and pass that
garbage
along and care nothing of

potential carnage along the way.
"Oh, that's their problem."
Awesome attitude,
Marla.
Anyhow, I realize I certainly
can't persuade you.
I'm praying for you, though,
that you would stop reading
garbage*.*
I guess I don't know
if you're still spreading
garbage*,*
but I'm praying that you won't.

(words his, **bold font** mine)

clapback

a very strong and well-observed
comeback—spoken or written—to criticism

one so fierce it utterly destroys
and owns its target

see also: clapback lite

a clapback minus the utter destruction
with some funny sprinkled in

still spreading garbage?

oh, absolutely
very much so
no doubt about it

opening up garbage
can after garbage can
of theological worms

and going fishing

see appendix b

there are a handful of / garbage books
that if I could just get / every conservative

Christian to read / I think we'd solve
some serious shit / I mean crap

can confirm

"I've heard it said that
there is no more hateful
person than a Christian who
thinks you've got your
theology wrong."

—**Sarah Bessey**

brother-in-Christ exhorts some more

I have talked with many of you
cautiously about the danger
of reading mounds of books and
the possibility of them subtly
removing the authority of
Scripture in your hearts.

It is not of God to allow false
teaching into your minds.
He has made that clear.
My exhortation for you is to wake
up and realize that the Enemy is on
an all-out assault, masterfully using all
forms of media to introduce doubts and
heresies that shipwreck lives and render
us useless for the Kingdom of God!

Shut them off!
Quit reading them!
Quit listening to them!
Quit "liking" them!
Quit sharing them!
Quit excusing them!

Tune your ears to listen only
to the Good Shepherd!

sigh

imagine thinking
you can't read
a single word
from a source
other than the Bible
or your life is
shipwrecked
and rendered
useless

bulletproof vest / cable knit sweater

growing up I heard a lot of war language
when it came to the christian faith it was

all about defense, put on the full armor of God
swords and shields and breastplates and such

standing firm, letting nothing penetrate

Brené Brown says that, out of self-protection,
we choose "uncertainty over curiosity, armor
over vulnerability, knowing over learning."

and she's a thousand percent right

but we don't have to trade in our Bibles for Brené
we just need to cherry pick a different verse

therefore, as God's chosen people,
holy and dearly loved,
clothe yourselves with compassion,
kindness, humility, gentleness and patience

that's some armor I can get behind

my favorite preacher

"You think your pain
and your heartbreak
are unprecedented in
the history of the world,

but then you read.

It was books that taught me
that the things that tormented
me most were the very things
that connected me with
all the people who were alive,
who had ever been alive."

—James Baldwin

don't smell my breff!

just three years old, she wasn't supposed to
steal peppermints from her dad's dresser

when interrogated, she denied it, lips pursed
tight, eyes wide with fear, backing away

don't smell my breff!

the gatekeepers stand with their absolute truth
eyes narrowed in fear, lips pursed tight

don't trust science! / don't listen to the media!
don't read any books! / don't ask questions!

don't trust your emotions! / don't question authority!
don't look too close! / don't poke the beast!

don't smell my breff!

sola scriptura

THE BIBLE ONLY
no trash books
by other
non-God-breathed authors
well of course except
for these holy anointed
white men
who are mostly dead now
but got everything right
and probably would have been
in the Bible too
if God had been so inclined
to publish a
second volume

difference

Jesus didn't rush in
to keep people

from breaking God's laws
and hurting God

Jesus rushed in
to keep people

from using God's laws
to hurt God's people

plank eye

leave this person alone

widow
adulteress
prostitute
children
woman with all the husbands
hungry one picking grain

Jesus said

and worry about
your own damn self

role model

Jesus was accused
of being a friend of sinners

have you ever been
accused of that?

or have you only ever been
the one doing the accusing?

unwelcome in their hometown

weird how prophets in the Bible
are almost always defined

by the way their own people
mock and ridicule them

now you've got people quoting Paul
and ignoring the prophets altogether

because their words make people
squirm and do not mesh in any way

with white male American Christianity
and its quest for domination and power

off script

no one can give me
a solid answer
or explanation
for all the times
Jesus says
odd/funny/disconcerting
things like sell all your stuff and
give the money to the poor
or don't mind the rules, you
can pick grain on the
Sabbath and oh, I'm going
to heal this person while
I'm at it even though
God's law explicitly
forbids it

what does the goat say?

when you studied for the final and did
everything right, then you find out you're

getting graded on feeding the hungry
and clothing the naked and giving water

to the thirsty and inviting in the stranger
and visiting the sick and the prisoner

and not in fact on church attendance and
Bible reading and pious prayers and not saying fuck

and policing other people's sexuality
what in the actual hellfire is happening here?

my first clue

should have been
when all you
wanted to talk about
was Jesus' death
and didn't give a
shit about his life

false dichotomy

I care about truth and
Marla just cares about justice

it's not either/or
I care deeply about both

can you even have one
without the other?

same

"Talking heads
dissecting apologetics
stopped inspiring me
a few years ago."

—Jen Hatmaker

imago dei

you defend God

and I defend people
created in God's image

why would God
need defending?

but I worked so hard on it

"I don't think
God is glorified
by tightly crafted
arguments wielded
as weaponry."

—Sarah Bessey

omniscient

isn't it ironic
that a mysterious
and infinite God
whose ways are
higher than ours
is so figure-out-able
to the point that you
know exactly what that
God wants each person
to do and how?

blurred

where is the line
between trying to be more
like
God
and trying to
be
God?
because I think
you've / they've / we've
crossed it

no thank you

love the sinner
hate their

queerness
Blackness
Muslim-ness
otherness

why does that not
seem like any kind of
love at all?

christian logic

some
times
love
feels
like
hate
she
said

clang clang

if you're not
loving
then I don't
care if you're
right
and there's really no
right
without love
anyway

correction

people are sinning against God
and must be stopped

no

churches and governments and Christians
especially Christians
are sinning against *people*
and must be stopped

zealotry

that fiery passion for
saving souls from
eternal damnation is
serving me well on
my quest to eradicate
supremacy in all its
insidious forms—

white
cis
straight
male
american
christian

cut off

five years since I've seen you
you and your husband disowned me

refused to see me unless I repent
of my heresy which I won't do

I'll repent for sins I commit against
people, not for my refusal to sign off

on your long list of harmful beliefs
I hate that you made me choose between

a relationship with you and loving my
neighbor but that's what you did

I feel you

my friend Kay says she
experiences real grief
over relationships that can't
survive her authenticity

apologetics ad infinitum

you and I both know we could debate
theology back and forth until the end of time

each of us having the perfect verses to
prove our every point but there is such

a wide chasm between our philosophies
of life that will most likely never be bridged

you aren't willing to step toward me and
no way in hell am I ever going back

shake it off

even Jesus couldn't change everybody's mind
so how in the hell would I stand a chance?

back of my hand

aside from the flat-out absurd
almost all of the rhetoric folks use

to dispute me is the same exact stuff
I clubbed liberals with back in the day

so I'm rarely caught off guard like
"wow, I never thought of it like that"

I thought of it just like that for so long

unfair advantage

I have yet to meet a conservative christian
that wants to fight with me

who has read (or written) as many
conservative christian books as I have

licentiousness

you just want / to make the Bible
say whatever you want so / you can

sin without guilt

yeah not really interested in lying /
cheating / killing / stealing / even sex

maybe cussing but / I keep looking for
don't say fuck in the Bible / and I

can't seem to / find the verse

maybe it's maybelline

maybe I'm playing devil's advocate
maybe it's a rebellious phase
maybe deconstruction is just a trend

maybe I woke up to the truth

talking heads

I have zero interest in engaging in
a theological debate with you

the only reason I would fight to
persuade you of anything at all

is because I believe your beliefs
are toxic and harming our neighbors

belief in a young earth isn't toxic in itself
but it's based on a belief that the Bible

is to be taken literally / that literalist
view leads to beliefs that oppress people

and I can't stand by and let that happen
otherwise, believe whatever you want

because I literally (*literally*) do not care

answers in Genesis

your insistence on believing that the
earth is just 6000 years old because

"the Bible says so" is beyond my
comprehension, not just because it

makes zero logical scientific sense
but the Bible does not in fact say so

the fact that I believed this for so long
is one of my greatest embarrassments

you can't simply tally genealogies
to get a 6000-year-old planet

genealogies skip generations and individual
names often represent entire people groups

the math (and common sense) just don't add up

the age-old science/faith quandary

"We understand today that the
physical universe is bigger and
older and operates very differently
than how the biblical writers, and
all other ancient people, thought.
Many Christians stumble over this,
thinking they are showing respect
for the Bible and obeying God by
making the biblical story mesh with
modern science, or rejecting modern
science entirely in favor of God's Word."

—Pete Enns

there's no santa claus?

I remember the first time a fellow Christian
suggested the biblical creation story was a myth

not literally true and oh so similar to other
creation myths told by other civilizations

in the same time frame, it's not even the first
or oldest and the parallels/similarities are uncanny

and what in the hell do you do with the idea that
your one true story in a world of mythology might

just be one more literary device in a giant collection?

Galileo

a few centuries ago,
excommunicated
from the Church for
heresy
had the audacity
to claim
that the earth
revolved around the
sun
and not the other way
around
which could not possibly be
true
because we all know that
the Bible
literally
says the sun
is the body
that does the
moving

solis

if the Bible was
"God-breathed"
i.e. God told them
what to write,
did God think the
sun revolved
around the earth?
did God
create the universe
then forget
how it worked?

good point

"Genesis says we were formed
from dust, but cosmology tells
us that you don't get dust—unless
you have stars first. Without dust,
you don't have the material to make
trees or humans. There were no
trees in our universe before
there were stars."

—Science Mike McHargue

say what?

you know that Satan
is never mentioned
in the creation story
right?

the Bible only ever says
"snake" or "serpent"
and you know that
talking snakes were a
common literary device
used at that time,
right?

file this under:
things your pastor
won't tell you
but Rob Bell will

oh, I see why

evolution is so threatening
books are so dangerous
Rob Bell is so menacing

because doubts and growth are
unmanageable / uncontainable
uncontrollable / unchainable

and you need something
safe / secure / certain / final
that can't slip away from you

wrong word

when the Bible you're holding in your hand
references "the word of God," it's not talking

about the actual Bible you're holding in your hand

that wasn't a thing yet when those words were written
some dudes pieced together your Bible centuries later

you know about this, right?

"Books were left out,
writings were edited,
things were added,
decisions were made about
which books belonged, and
eventually the library of books
we know to be the Bible came to be
THE BIBLE."

—Rob Bell

in the beginning was the word

I don't know that Jesus
would have loved our Bible

if he'd stuck around long
enough to see it published

John 14:12

Jesus told his followers that
anyone who believes in him

would do even greater things than
he did so the Bible wasn't the end

greater things were yet to come

but you ignore him and insist
the Bible is the greatest thing

the greatest only definitive conclusive
decisive incontrovertible final thing

I'm going with Jesus on this one

red letters

I am going to heaven / to prepare a place for you
you can't come / but don't be sad

I'm sending someone / to take my place
I call him / THE KING JAMES BIBLE

did you know?

the Gnostic Gospels that
didn't make the canon cut

had a ton of divine feminine
influence in them

can't imagine why the
white European men who

put the Bible together
opted to leave those out

not women

he who writes the story
controls the glory
and who wrote the Bible?

all the king's horses

when you post these things
on Facebook, she writes,
you set yourself up as a
teacher of theology and
you owe us a more
detailed explanation of
blah blah blah
blah blah blah

hon, this is *Facebook*

I am perched on my own
damn wall like a backyard
Humpty Dumpty
just swinging my legs
and saying stuff
that comes to mind

the idea that I owe you
something, a single thing
any damn thing at all
is so absurd and hilarious
I can't stop laughing
and have to hold on tighter

lest I have a great fall

facebook

explain yourself!
they say

you owe us!
they say

in fact
I don't

burn, David

you like to stir the pot

well yeah so do all good cooks
what happens if you don't?

a couple things: all the good stuff
will be unevenly distributed

in one or two bites or bowls
while the other people just get broth

or the soup burns, gets stuck to the bottom
you lose a bunch of it, the rest is inedible

and the pot's a bitch to clean later

who am I, Captain Marvel?

you need to be careful
leading people astray
sending people to hell

I literally had no idea I had this
kind of power daaaaammmmmn

but you can't just

watch
me

the other cheeky

you need to / forgive these people
who have slandered / and hurt you

oh, I plan on it / have it on
the calendar / for next September

damn it

May 5, 2019 Facebook post
the day after Rachel died

I hate hate hate the idea of a world
without Rachel Held Evans in it,
damn it. Life is so unfair.

empathy / sentiment echoed / we loved her too

and then that one person / always that one person

Why are you swearing as a Christian, that's
what I'm wondering?? That's not Christ like
by any means and not a Godly example.

oh, the deep deep irony of her response
giving me a glimpse into the cruel future

where we navigate conservative Christian
bullshit without Rachel as our guide

DAMN IT.

what in the hell?

if you're reading this as someone who
has never been a part of the conservative

evangelical world and you are baffled
mystified as to why the word *damn*

could possibly be any kind of big deal in
any imaginable way, stick with me

got a whole alternate universe to show you

cleanse

I used to copy and
paste shitty things
annoying people said to
me on Facebook so I
could refute the hell out
of them in a book
someday, it felt
really good to
delete them all just
now and wipe them
from my memory

(okay I kept a few)

high road

a friend said he didn't want to
spend time bashing those who

have thrown rocks at him, he wants
to honor those who've encouraged him

I love that and I too have so many
people to honor, but first, some rocks

just kidding, no rocks, well maybe a few
tiny pebbles tossed in their general direction

you know, kind of like sarcastic confetti

thank you, Rachel, once again

when random folks come
out of the facebook woodwork

to pick fights and ask
annoying rhetorical questions

here's a brilliant RHE quote
to copy/paste as a reply:

"I'm no longer ready to give an answer about everything.
Sometimes I'm not ready because I feel that an answer
does not do justice to the seriousness or complexity
of the question. Sometimes I'm not ready to give an
answer because I honestly don't know what the best one is.
Sometimes I'm not ready to give an answer because I can tell
that the person asking doesn't really want one anyway."

—Rachel Held Evans

daughters of Eve

I haven't done the
Latin, but I
imagine there's a
reason heretic starts
with her

man cave

a smidge confused as to why God
would make removal of penis skin

the definitive sign that people have
chosen to follow him and by people

I mean the half of humanity born
with that particular appendage

exegete and applicate

let this evening's
bible study commence

open your copy of the word
to 1 Corinthians 7:18

was a man already circumcised when he was called?

he should not become uncircumcised. (NIV)
he should not undo his circumcision. (CSB)
let him not seek to remove the marks of circumcision. (ESV)
he should not try to reverse it. (NLT)

so um I guess don't try to patch
your penis / just cut your losses?

modesty

when the Bible says *modest*
does it mean *humble, moderate*

or does it mean *don't show too much thigh*
or any part of that line between your boobs?

because Peter wrote
your beauty should not come
from outward adornment,
such as elaborate hairstyles and
the wearing of gold jewelry or fine clothes

but the youth pastor says
it's about your cleavage
making good Christian boys
want to rape you

what's a girl to do?

tiny violin

imagine how tough
it's got to be for
ultra-conservative Christian
men
to see their
long-bowed,
dutiful,
do-everything-for-their-husband
wives
start to wake up
and smell the patriarchy

submission

so God wants me / to be silent in church
and pray / with my head covered

and ask my husband questions / at home

should I be lucky enough / to have one
and smart enough to / think of any

is that how the complementarianism / goes?

misnomer

peanut butter and jelly
ketchup and mustard

those are complementary
there's no hierarchy

it's not pb on top, j on the bottom
they're different, but equally important

biblical complementarianism isn't equal
the man is always more important

she's the ketchup to his fries
the mustard to his hot dog

he's the main course, the big deal
it's more like condimentarianism

pillow talk

once upon a time she read my marriage book
but hated my second book about sex

*your first book had so much Scripture
in every chapter, this one has hardly any*

so weird how folks think an ancient Bible
is somehow a 21st century marriage manual

regrets

I did a hell of a lot of submitting
to my husband over the years

because I thought it was biblical
when really I was kowtowing to his

insecurities, ignorance, unfairness, and
demand for respect when he hadn't earned it

turtleneck it

why do conservative Christian men
insist on the subjugation of women
in the name of godly biblical womanhood?

fear

they know our power
tell us it's evil

button it up
cover it up
bottle it up
shut it down

we do have a power
that can take men down
but it's not below the neck

it's above it

Jesus Feminist

"At the core, feminism simply consists
of the radical notion that women are people, too.

Patriarchy is not God's dream for humanity.
It never was; it never will be."

—Sarah Bessey

anyone?

show me where
the whole
godly
biblical
complementarian
marriage
thing
is modeled
by an
actual couple
in the Bible

on the other hand
I do see a lot of
polygamy and rape
and leaving your
wives and fishing nets
to follow Jesus
and Paul advising
singleness if
you want to be godly

least favorite christian quote

"Your greatest contribution
to the kingdom of God
may not be something you do
but someone you raise."

—Andy Stanley

a word for Andy Stanley

that's not a quote for *parents* / it's for *mothers*
no one is telling *men* their greatest contribution

to the kingdom is raising a kid who'll do great things
men get to do awesome stuff on their own

and it's really just a quote for mothers of *sons*
as a mom of daughters, fingers crossed that

they'll marry a kingdom contributor and
birth man-children who will do kingdom bigness

and my childless women friends / sorry about your luck
you've got nothing to contribute to the kingdom at all

girls can do anything

for all the conservative evangelical
Christian theology my parents imparted

to me growing up that I have spent the
last decade undoing, unraveling, unlearning,

and unbelieving, I do not remember one
single instance where they led me to believe

that my gender kept me from doing anything
my precocious mind and wild heart desired

as a girl and a young woman, the entire world
was mine to do whatever I wanted with

fishing, mud bakery, collecting baseball cards,
reading, baling hay, watching football games

playing school, writing poems, running, mowing
solving calculus problems, working at a motorcycle plant

thank you, Mom and Dad, for not living out
the gender hierarchy taught by the church

inflation

bummer when your
whiteness
maleness
Christian-ness
starts to
lose its
perceived value
makes sense that
you're acting out

false narrative

human nature has us / identifying with the Bible's
oppressed / but an honest assessment shows we're

actually the Egyptians Babylonians Romans Pharisees

the story of U.S. Christianity is / not one of persecution
no matter what we tell ourselves / it's one of power

and wanting our religion to be the / law of the land
hate to break it to you but / we're the bad guys

on evangelicals as the "persecuted minority"

"I'll admit I was disappointed when I
learned that something like 85 percent
of Americans identify themselves as
Christians. Knowing you're in the
majority makes the whole thing a
lot less dramatic and sexy."

—Rachel Held Evans

mighty warrior god

no wonder European Christians thought
it was a-okay to slaughter Indigenous peoples

standing in the way of their Manifest Destiny
when the God they follow seemingly ordered

his people to commit genocide of men, women,
and babies without even batting a holy eye

one nation under god

the colonizers were Christians
the scalpers were Christians
the enslavers were Christians
the rapists were Christians
the Confederate traitors were Christians
the residential school teachers were Christians
the KKK were Christians
the lynchers were Christians
the segregationists were Christians
the war criminals were Christians
the mass shooters were Christians
the insurrectionists were Christians

the very good gospel

"I had to face a hard truth: my limited,
evangelical understanding of the gospel
had nothing to say about 16,000 Cherokees
and four other sovereign nations whose people
were forcibly removed from their lands.
And it had nothing to say to my own ancestors
who were enslaved in South Carolina."

—Lisa Sharon Harper

original sin / 150-years-ago sin

why are we automatically sinners
because the first man sinned

and we each have to make it right
pray a prayer, accept Jesus

but our recent ancestors' sins—
genocide of Indigenous peoples

and enslavement of Africans
to name just two of so many

have nothing to do with us
and simply aren't our concern?

we have it backward

"Indigenous peoples are labeled idol worshipers and animists because we have an understanding with the earth and the creatures around us that much of the white, Western church has lost."

—**Kaitlin Curtice**

assimilate or go home

I read this book where the author spent
10 years befriending Muslims and did not

convert a single one and instead of giving
up and moving on she decides to just keep

being friends with them and eating and drinking
with them and talking to them and learning

their stories and making them rainbow confetti
cakes and barely even trying to save their souls

from eternal damnation and then has the nerve to
talk about all the ways these Muslims "taught

her about the gospel" excuse me, say what?
(this exact same beautiful thing happened to me)

abbey lane

for one hard beautiful year we lived
in an apartment complex with refugee

neighbors from Somalia, Eritrea, Nepal
none of us had much to our names, but they

shared everything they had—homes, meals
sambusa and shaah and laughs and friendship

their love literally changed our lives

our beautiful Muslim neighbors

"Don't be caught off guard when people
show up from outside whatever system
or institution or religion or perspective
or doctrine or worldview or culture
you've created and they have something
profound and good to give to you."

—Rob Bell

when foreign becomes familiar

people of other religions and their gods
scared me from far away, so I got closer

visiting holy sacred Hindu and Buddhist
temples and statues in Cambodia

learning from a friend who was
studying ancient Hebraic scrolls

fasting with my Muslim friends for
Ramadan, then breaking fast together

honoring our Cambodian friends'
ancestors, like my son-in-law's parents

going to a child dedication celebration
and dancing with my Eritrean friends

attending a Catholic mass in Cambodia
and many many beautiful weddings

eating meals in the homes of my Somali,
Eritrean, Cambodian, Thai, Mexican friends

getting blessed by a Buddhist priest at
my daughter's Khmer engagement ceremony

God is so much bigger than I thought

on strangers and sojourners

when you, a Christian, tell me on Facebook that
Jesus warned us about wolves in sheep's clothing

and he was talking about illegal immigrants
then I know you don't know any immigrants

or Jesus

you love foreigners as long as they
stay within their own map lines

you love missionaries, *here's $20, go love on people*
try to convert them, save their poor souls

and for god's sake make sure they stay
over there where they belong

the colonization ends here

the day I decided to drop
the proselytizer from my title

and just be the humanitarian part
was a very very good day

not everyone thought so

indoctrination

we made the overdue decision to
stop sharing the gospel with kiddos at

our Bamboo Libraries in Cambodia
and some people were super unhappy

we compared it to dropping off your
child at your local library storytime

would you want a Hindu or Muslim
teacher reading to your kiddos from

their sacred texts, telling them it's truth,
having them pray a prayer to accept it?

that's different, people told me
we have the truth, they don't

then share your "truth" with the parents
and let them decide what to tell their kids

the same way you'd expect people of
other faiths to respect you and your family

notes from a former colonizer

I loved missionary stories as a kid

I'd like to believe it was my compassionate nature
that caused them to hold such appeal and not that I

was already invested in a white savior complex
and a colonizer mentality at such a young age

how many "missionary" stories did I read from the
perspective of those who were invaded and violated?

zero

it was all framed as heathens vs. truth-bearing heroes of faith

how lucky they were to have been discovered by
these white angels of mercy and salvation and rightness

maybe I'll write a whole book about this someday

biblical racism

I've only ever met one person
who literally believed in
"the curse of Ham"

her grandson was dating a Black woman
(I married another one of her grandsons)
and she didn't approve

they're cursed, you know

excuse me, what?

*through Ham, Noah's son
he sinned and now they're all cursed*

I thought I was used to her stories
her superstitious beliefs
but nothing like this
this was different, evil

I was horrified, we argued
my eyes were opened wide wide
and our relationship was
never the same again

#TrayvonMartin

why aren't my white friends talking
about this? a Black friend asked

in her Feb. 2012 facebook post
taken aback / I didn't know

Trayvon Martin, a Black teen
murdered / he was just 17

another senseless unjust death
of someone unarmed and Black

by a man taking the "law"
into his own damn hands

I began to look / to read
to learn / heartsick, broken

his death was my catalyst
changed me, changed everything

but his mama doesn't have
her baby and never will

Trayvon you woke me up
and you'll never wake up

and everything in the world

is wrong wrong wrong with that

dear white peacemaker

"I'm going to say something that you're not going to like: If you pull away from the Black Lives Matter movement, which is arguably the most impactful expression of the fight for human dignity of this moment, because it comes in a package you don't like, then you don't have enough proximity to the pain of white supremacy. If you resist aligning yourself with Black Lives Matter and the conversation about racism turns into a fun thought experiment or a lively debate on Facebook about philosophical ideas and not a visceral pain in your gut for the extreme loss of life and liberty for Black people in America, then you are in danger of worshiping a god of Intellect and not Jesus, the humble suffering servant. Jesus, who was persecuted because he defended people when everyone else wanted him to defend their ideas or politics."

—Osheta Moore

amen and amen

"We can disagree and
still love each other
unless your disagreement
is rooted in my oppression
and denial of my humanity
and right to exist."

—Robert Jones, Jr.

Note: Mr. Jones (@sonofbaldwin) shared this on Twitter with this important caveat: "This a Black quote with Black intent and Black impact for Black people. It's great if you find some universality in it, but recognize its core is Black. Thank you."

the color of compromise

if every white U.S. Christian would
just read this phenomenal book

I could retire from my unpaid gig as
missionary to the white American church

you would think that evangelical
Christianity and antiracism could co-exist

I have yet to see any compelling evidence

more amens

"The festering wound of racism
in the American church must be
exposed to the oxygen of truth
in order to be healed."

—**Jemar Tisby**

all *you* need is Jesus

salvation is the most important thing
at least the slaves had Jesus, you know?

and freedom from oppression is a nice bonus
but if that doesn't work out for you on earth

don't worry, you get to go to heaven

of course, *I* get to enjoy all the days of my life
but everybody else can wait until they die

say it louder

"How can the church be the answer to
Christian supremacy and white supremacy
in the United States when it is also an
instigator and product of this mangled history?

To get a better handle on the captivity of the
church to supremacist identities, mindsets,
and ways of living, we need to know our past.

If we can begin to see the supremacist
mindsets woven into American Christianity,
we can begin pulling on the threads and
unraveling the idolatry."

—Drew G. I. Hart

white girl learning

I've learned so much the past few years
about racial injustice and white supremacy

I could learn for 50 more years and still
not learn it all—or even come close

it's hard work but necessary work
humbling work but holy work

it's my passion through and through
and I'm navigating what it looks like for a

white woman to share her thoughts while
staying in her lane / not centering herself

unlearn, relearn, make things right, restitution
reparations, land acknowledgments, land back

supporting the work and art of our Black siblings
Indigenous siblings, other siblings of color

restore what locusts have long devoured
and humbly admit we're the locusts

God's name in vain

my mama always told me that
don't take God's name in vain
meant never say *oh my god*

but it really means don't say shit like

God told me to forcefully drive you off
your land and kill you and your children
with diseases and residential schools

God told me that Black people are less
human than white people and it's good
for me to own them like animals

God told me to invade your country, pillage
your diamonds, cover your nakedness
and force you to convert to my religion

God told me to overlook Trump's moral
failure and incessant cruelty and vote
for him so Christians can have power

God told me (I prayed long and hard about this)
to leave my wife and kids and go back
to Cambodia to be with my lover

slapping God's name on violence and evil
is vain vain vain vain vain vain vain

love wins

the great and mighty and
holy controversial Batman
Rob Bell
wrote a book about hell
a decade ago
I bought it on a
whim, read a third of it,
couldn't stomach it, and
threw it away

a haiku for Rob Bell seven years later

I dug your book out
of the trash and hungrily
devoured it whole

too much too fast

my book might be one you
throw away now and pick up later

part of me wanted to ease into
the parts I knew would piss you off

but that's a lot of paper and
who has that kind of time?

listen to yourself

if there's no hell,
then what's the point
of being a Christian?

sad but the truest

"Some Christians
are more offended
by the idea of everyone
going to heaven
than by the idea of everyone
going to hell."

—Rachel Held Evans

inherently good

assuming I'm only moral because God
will send me to hell if I'm not is insulting

we're taught we're wretched sinners who
would only ever choose sin if left to our own

devices but I call bullshit because I know
I'm a goodhearted person who wants to

love my neighbor and myself and don't
need a hell-gun held to my head to do it

give 'em hell

Love Wins is such / a brilliant book title
and so offensive / to Christians who must

have forgotten that God is love / and love
winning means God wins / but they think

God winning / means all the losers have to burn

I saw this meme

blond Jesus knocks on a wooden door
the dialogue's in word bubbles

Jesus: let me in!
Person: why?
Jesus: so I can save you.
Person: from what?
Jesus: from what I'm going to do to you if you don't let me in.

excuse me, what?

"I hope hell is some kind
of eternal annihilation."

—a Christian in my fb comments

nope

you expect me to
believe that my
generous kind-hearted
Muslim neighbor
is going to hell
while my racist
self-centered
elderly relative is
on his way to heaven?
I don't buy it

once upon a time

"Telling a story about a God
who inflicts unrelenting punishment
on people because they didn't
do or say or believe the correct things
in a brief window of time called life
isn't a very good story."

—Rob Bell

fabulous news

the gospel is
the good news
that God is with you
for you
loves you
and you are inherently
unconditionally
worthy of that love

wait a second
you forgot the part
about hell

no, God took care
of all that

and what part of

God created a place
of eternal fire to torture you
unless you do/say
all the right things

is good?

#goals

"At Homeboy Industries, we
seek to tell each person this
truth: they are exactly what
God had in mind when God
made them—and then we
watch, from this privileged
place, as people inhabit
this truth."

—Father Gregory Boyle

some concerns

are the baddies
getting into heaven
just because they said
a prayer

and is there free will
in heaven

and will they be just as awful
up there
as they were
down here

because I would like
to speak to the landlord
about this before
I move in

things that make you go hmm

Paul *literally* said it's better
for men *not* to marry

yet here we sit touting marriage
as holy, godly, a cherished institution

Paul *literally* said marriage is a
distraction from kingdom work

yet nobody is decrying marriage ministries
and conferences and sermons and books

but bring up *racism* and the knee-jerk response?
well, that's a distraction from the gospel

extrapolation

extending something to an unknown
situation by assuming a continued
trend in a certain direction

the trend of the new testament
is more and more freedom

freedom from circumcision
freedom to eat foods
previously thought unclean

freedom for women to play
important roles in the kingdom

what's next? freedom for men to
wear their hair long if they want to?

freedom for women to ask questions in
church freely like men do?

getting rid of our slaves?
two women getting married?

so many many options

we can do this

it seems we've lost our imaginations
our ability to envision what might be next

what things in the Bible might mean
for us in today's changing world

we're able to do that in some areas
but we fight it so hard in others

why?

dialectic

the art of investigating
or discussing the truth
of opinions

I first learned this word
from the great Audre Lorde
and I love it

a third way

you're either
a slave to Christ
or a slave to sin

or I could just be free

mystery

I don't know
exactly
what God
is
yet
but I know
what God
is
not

and I can
tell you
that I will
never
ever
ever

go back to
that horrid God
you made up

ode to Uncle Grayson

everything that made you
a black sheep in our family
when I was growing up
you fighting for

gay rights
civil rights
human rights

makes you my hero now

crucify her

she affirms gay marriage because it's the
easy road and she just wants to be popular

easy road. popular.

you have clearly never been on the wrong side
of a massive gang of angry, jilted evangelicals

hell hath no fury

god and the gay christian

I assumed that anyone who affirmed
homosexuality just ignored the parts

of the Bible that address it, I didn't
expect to read a book by someone who

not only didn't gloss over those passages
but studied them more thoroughly critically

deeply smartly historically biblically
than I'd ever dreamed of doing

ix nay on the ex gay

I've read books by two "former lesbians"
and couldn't help but notice that neither

claims God took away their gayness, just
convicted them they needed to marry men

their life, their choice, but it's harmful to
preach that, insisting it's the only way

I believe God celebrates you for who you are,
not forces you to live a fake life to "honor God"

I know so many beautiful gay Christian couples
and I absolutely see God in their love

sodomy

every good Christian knows why
Sodom was destroyed, right?

two words: gay sex

Ezekiel 16:49-50:

now this was the sin of your sister Sodom:
she and her daughters were arrogant, overfed

and unconcerned; they did not help the poor and
needy. They were haughty and did detestable things

before me. Therefore I did away with them
as you have seen

two words: wait what?

pray the gay away

I know so many gay people who
hated themselves as kids (and adults)
because they thought they were bad

they prayed hundreds, thousands of
prayers for God to take away the gay
but God looked the other way

he said this out loud

yes I believe it's better
for a child to rot and die
in an orphanage than to be
adopted by two gay men

—an American worship leader at a church in Cambodia

as long as you're celibate

we're very loving here
(not to be confused with affirming)
and you don't need to
feel shame about *being* gay
just about *acting* on the gay
just like straight folks
shouldn't lust after
each other and think about
sex before we're married except it's
fine for us to daydream about the
future and hold hands and innocently
cuddle on the couch while
watching a movie but
you can't even do that
sorry you're screwed
no, we didn't say *you can screw*
we said *you're screwed* sorry
we still love you though
we're very loving here

Acts 15

some Gentiles are converted to Christianity
some Jewish believers say they have to be circumcised

Peter says *yeah we're not going to unnecessarily*
burden non-Jewish people who turn to the master

they've got the same holy spirit we do

what if there are gay Christians but some straight
believers say they have to become un-gay first

and we say *yeah we're not going to unnecessarily*
burden non-heterosexual people who turn to the master

come one, come all, come gay, stay that way!

silence speaks volumes

Jesus was so super fired up serious
about the gays being bad and evil

that he never said a single word about them

July 6, 2019

if you don't like the "sinful" way I love and affirm gay people
but don't have any gay friends

if you don't like the way I "celebrate" Muslims
but don't have any Muslim friends

if you don't like the way I "focus too much on racial injustice"
but don't have any Black friends

then all your many many many many many many
words are like clanging gongs of nothingness to me

quick question

so, the verse in Galatians that says
there is neither male nor female

how do we interpret that *literally*?

we're all equal?
complementarianism is out?
there's no longer a gender binary?
same sex marriage is cool now?
trans is beautiful?
women can wear the pants?
and talk in church? even preach?
and do whatever the hell men can do?

so many glorious options
I choose Z all of the above

seriously

so are we doing away with the
gender hierarchy or the gender binary?

or both? I vote both

a love poem to my queer siblings

I see you over there being awesome
and I celebrate you for all that you are

I celebrate every part of you you've been told
to hide / diminish / get rid of / pray away

you are not and have never been an abomination
you are and have always been a beautiful creation

you are so freaking generous, forgiving me
for all the years I lived in harmful ignorance

I will fight for you to have every single right
I have as a straight cis person in this country

and I will fight to open people's eyes to the fact
that we have been taught lies our whole lives

I love you and I love your queerness
so so so very very very much much much

love,
Marla

good fruit / bad fruit

there's a lot of talk
about fruit in the Bible

you know a tree by
the fruit it bears

you know if someone
has the holy spirit in them
if you see this fruit:

love / joy / peace / patience / goodness
kindness / gentleness / faithfulness / self-control

you'll know Jesus' disciples
by their love

and all the talk of speaking in tongues
of angels and knowing all of everything

and having faith that moves mountains but
all of it is bullshit without love, without fruit

the fruit of homophobia, nationalism, misogyny
racism, xenophobia, and patriarchy in the church

is nasty and rotten / throw it out

Jesus and John Wayne

I'd never read a book that
summarized so succinctly

my growing-up years in a
conservative evangelical family

how'd she get in my living room
pulling books off the shelf one by one

telling me the truth about these white
conservative christian male authors

and their quest for power and authority
via toxic masculinity and gender roles

and racism and fear mongering and look
at all those receipts to back up her claims

by this point I'd figured much of it out
but she connected the dots to perfection

and I'm feeling pretty freaking angry

a nod to 45

not keen to give you / much space in my book much like
my ex-in-laws / and angry white dudes from facebook

(well, there's a three-way Venn diagram overlap for you)

so I'll say that / evangelicals' support of you is gross
and disappointing and will / ultimately lead a buttload

of people away from / the christian faith

a person can't align themselves / with both you and Jesus
no matter what they say / with their mouths

and the rest of us know it / (they do too)

you're not the problem / 45
you just revealed the evil / at the core

and for that I give you / the only
sincere thank you / you will ever get from me

do you still believe in god?

well, that really depends on what
you mean by god / as I've already said

if your god condones a man / like Donald Trump
then I want nothing to do with / your god

dead inside

when you talk
about your
god
nothing comes alive in
me, that's
how I know it's
not the real
true one

toxic

some people turn their back
on the faith
because they've
been hurt

I turned my back
on the faith
because other people
were being hurt

your god / my god

bores me to tears / awes me to tears
makes you his slave / sets me free

places men over women / laughs at that absurdity
is a He with a capital H / is beyond gender

welcomes cruelty in his name / is love, always love
sends you to hell for non-compliance / is love, always love

demands and demands / is love, always love
is dead to me / is love, always love

one iota

as a first year teacher I taught
a unit on Greek mythology

we set the Greek alphabet
to the tune of the ABC song

alpha beta gamma delta
epsilon zeta eta theta iota...

years later, I taught my girls
... kappa lambda mu nu psi...

years after that, my youngest
decided to learn Greek on her own

like 13-year-olds do

hey Mom that's not actually
how you say those letters

she tried to reteach me the
correct pronunciation but

that song is stuck fast in my head

it would have been a lot easier, she said
if you'd never learned it the wrong way

no kidding

real or not real?

it feels like we
just broke out of
The Matrix

found out our lives
were scripted on the set of
The Truman Show

realized *The Good Place*
was really
The Bad Place

I'm skeptical
of every
little thing now

raw

all these years later
it's tempting to turn
every poem into a shrug

light, carefree, you tried to hurt
me but you couldn't
nah nah nah nah boo boo

but you could
and you did
and it still hurts

vulnerable

who cares? is the vibe I'm after, unbothered
unaffected by all I've lost since speaking my truth

I'd rather be admired, envied, than pitied
but it's not the whole story if I leave out the tears

a lot of my wounds have become scars
but some of them are still bleeding

I forgive you

I still can't believe someone I loved
so deeply could have been so cruel

but I forgive you, love you (and pity you)

you're in a prison of your own making
and mistakenly calling it freedom

I know you think God's love is a painful love,
a punishing love, a love that feels like hate

I hope someday you'll realize that's not true
that it's a distorted image of what God really is

God's love is a big love, an expansive love
a beautiful and extravagant and wild love

God is love and God's love feels like love

this is the part where

my husband of 22 years leaves me
unexpectedly and I find out four

months later that he's been cheating
on me for the past four years

but that, my friends, is another book
and there will absolutely be another book

there was no miracle

we actually truly believed that
God had healed my husband

of his crippling mental illness
three years post-heart attack

that we were free to go, to
serve God in a foreign land

but believing in "healing" and
not doing the necessary work

of actually healing his mind from
trauma came back to destroy us

raises hand

sorry but I'm not going to be able to go to church
anymore because 1 Corinthians 14:35 says that if

a woman desires to learn anything, she needs
to ask her husband at home because it's

disgraceful/shameful/improper for a woman
to speak in a church and I know myself

I'm gonna have a question and then what?

isn't that precious?

Augustine believed that men
were made in the image of God

and women could become that
image after they got married

so what happens after divorce?

screw it

when you've been deconstructing your
belief system for over a decade and now

aaaalll these Christians support a heinous man
and you move back to the States in the middle

of a pandemic and your husband leaves you and
then you find out he's a lying conniving adulterer

you wipe the tears, throw up your hands, grin
mischievously and say to hell with the filter

hook, line, and asshole

my history teachers were telling lies
my pastors were telling lies
my husband was telling lies

I hate that I was duped for so long

to my ex and evangelical christianity

you both wanted me to be less,
smaller, quieter, wanted me

to suppress who I really was
inside because it benefited you,

gave you power, made you look
good when you weren't, I'm a

better person, more me, on the
other side of both of you

been there done that

I will absolutely celebrate your marriage
but I don't ever want another one

and I will even celebrate your cool church
but I don't want another one of those either

music to my ears

I just bought this book
on your recommendation

p.s.
if you want a really good book
that ends with the author going
back to church and falling in love
with it all over again, read

Sarah Bessey's *Out of Sorts* or
RHE's *Searching for Sunday*

that doesn't happen
at the end
of my book

first words from you in two years

I'm so sorry
about Gabe

oh
please
you
divorced
me
first

circular reasoning

love your neighbor / as you love yourself
the Bible seems clear / just like you like it

but wait / you tell me
sometimes love / feels like hate

and I guess that makes / sense because
you use words like wretched / worm / rubbish

to describe yourself / and so why wouldn't you
use similar words to / describe your neighbor

and call it love?

the realest thing

"I do not believe I am describing a loss of faith in God here. Instead, I believe I am describing a loss of faith in the system that promised to help me grasp God not only by setting my feet on the right track but also by giving me the right language, concepts, and tools to get a hook in the Real Thing when I found it."

—Barbara Brown Taylor

"a God thing"

not only did my faith shift but my
language shifted right along with it

I stopped using hundreds of canned
phrases and added a few choice words

many of them with four letters and yes
the words from the can still trigger me

rethinking go-to metaphors

are we standing firm in our faith
or are we *cemented, frozen?*

strong and rooted and immovable?
or *constipated* and *stuck?*

I like the growing / changing / evolving
blossoming imagery better

make it make sense

why does God get praised for every good thing
but we're not supposed to blame God for the bad?

from now on I'm taking both credit and
responsibility for everything myself

of tears and tongues

what about the time I was standing in church
and fell to the concrete floor sobbing

and words and sounds and moaning
flew out of my mouth of their own accord

and for months after, whenever I sobbed
facedown on the floor, my tongue

took on a mind of her own

I don't know

and I'm cool
with that
so very cool

mine fit in a coin purse

"I cannot say for sure
when my reliable ideas
about God began to slip away,
but the big chest I used to
keep them in is smaller
than a shoebox now."

—Barbara Brown Taylor

weird

I get the same amount
of answered prayers
these days as I used to
get and I haven't prayed
in months

apatheist

a temporary label
I'm giving myself
while I take a break
from even caring
what I believe about God

(google informed me just now that
I did not in fact invent this word)

irrelevant

if I don't see love in someone's life
I really truly do not give a single damn

what they believe about Jesus'
death, burial, and resurrection

the whole spectrum

"People want
black-and-white
answers, but
Scripture is a
rainbow arch across
a stormy sky."

—Sarah Bessey

when I was a kid

I used to take everything off my bookshelf
out of my dresser and closet, dump it on my bed

then slowly, meticulously put back only the stuff
I really wanted to keep, the only problem was that I

was super indecisive so it took me a looooong time
to put stuff back and I'd get tired and stop and read

a book and without fail nighttime would come and
there would still be a huge pile on my bed so I'd

move it to the floor and put it all back on the bed
the next day and move it all to the floor the next

night repeat repeat repeat, pretty soon, everything
I owned just lived on the floor and I didn't even care

at some point, my dad came into my room with a rake
and raked all of my precious belongings into a pile and

told me to clean it all up or he'd throw them away, and
in my imperfect memory, I did, and I've kept things neat

ever since except when I haven't, now here I am
45 years old and I've taken all my beliefs accumulated

over decades, off my shelves and out of my drawers

and closets and piled it on my bed and I'm being careful

to only put back what is true and loving and
causes no harm but I always get tired before bedtime

no more slow-mo

I get that some don't like it when people
up ahead on the deconstruction journey

seem impatient with those who just started

you need to go slower
be more gentle
give them time

I hear you and would absolutely love to

but can you see what a privileged take that is
to think we have the luxury of going slowly

while the world burns down around us?

ten years ago was already too late for those
who needed us to wake up long before then

my comfort matters less than people's lives

front row seats to her mom's deconstruction show

people tell me I don't treat evangelicals very lovingly
that I beat them up because I think my beliefs are superior

I need to be more generous, gracious, soothing, kind

my oldest says: "Mom, you're not attacking other
people's beliefs, you're admitting you were wrong."

she's right / I am (admitting) / I was (wrong)

my end goal is love, confessing to harm, ditching
toxic beliefs, rewiring, making reparations

imploring those still causing damage to stop

Jesus didn't coddle arrogant dudes
wasn't gentle with religious folks

I'm not Jesus (obvs) / I won't do it perfectly
no one can agree what that looks like anyway

I'm open to criticism/suggestions but don't take
advice from anyone who hasn't done time in the arena

(shoutout to Teddy Roosevelt and Brené Brown)

I got your letter

four handwritten pages reminding me
I'm going to hell for my heresies

you added a new twist this time
said I hate God and Jesus and the church

that's a bit much, even for you

for the record, I own all my heresies
lucky for me, I no longer believe in hell

but I don't hate God, Jesus, nor the church
never have, never will, never said I did

my deconstructing journey began with love
well over a decade ago now

and love continues to be my driving force

I don't know how to make you see it

It breaks my heart that you refuse to trust
your intuition / feelings / desires because

you've been taught that your heart is evil
it's not / there are so many ways to follow it

where everyone is better because of you,
this amazing beautiful worthy creature

but you don't know how to see yourself that way
so how can you ever hope to love your neighbor?

if you think you're wretched and sinful and
there's not a lick of good to be found in you,

does God look at you and see that too? / did God

create the world, call it good, then one apple bite
and it's all trash until heaven? / what a sad story

why would a loving God demand incessant groveling
and belittling and self-hatred, call us worms?

God designed you, created you, called you good
I love you / God loves you / please love yourself

road trip

the sign said
heresy: 8 miles ahead

so I tightened the straps
on my backpack
and kept walking

it's been so fun to meet
so many fellow travelers
sharing stories and tears and snacks

and oh so many jokes
really funny jokes

if we can't have
a little fun on the road
to heresy, well, boo

flip the connotation switch

apostate
heretic
dissident
skeptic
renegade
iconoclast

these words all give me
warm fuzzies now

wrecking ball

when you're part of a harmful cult
you get out and warn others

and people accuse you of being
just as dogmatic as those in the cult

there's a reason Christians in power
fight hard against deconstruction

the system is in danger of crumbling
if it's toxic—and it is—let it fall

speak your truth

when you give voice
to what you feel and
know deep down inside

you give others
the courage they need
to do it too

he ain't kidding

"You can't take people where they
don't want to go. The thing that
you are so happy to be freed from
still works for some people. They
like it. It feels safe. It provides
meaning and security. So when you
challenge it and quote whoever you've
been reading lately and ask the questions
that opened new doors for you, they
do not find this energizing."

—**Rob Bell**

rubber gloves

I'm not here to take away
anyone's comforting beliefs

well, just the ones that harm others

we're good-hearted people, we're not
holding harmful beliefs on purpose

we often don't know they're harmful
until someone points it out

it's tempting to defend them
without examining them

but as I started digging deeper
I've found over and over again

that some of the very things that
brought me comfort over the years

are oppressive to others
like Ms. Maya Angelou said

"I did then what I knew how to do.
Now that I know better, I do better."

we don't have to land at the same
conclusions but we shouldn't leave

any stones unturned because we're
worried about our own personal comfort

not when our neighbors are hurting

don't be afraid

if your beliefs are solid,
they'll survive the scrutiny

if they're not,
isn't it better to know?

lofty

haven't quite
figured out
how to transcend
without looking down
on people,
will keep
at it and p.s. I'm
only accepting advice
from a handful of
people and you're
probably not one of
them, shoot, did I just do
it again?

this book

is me getting all the
rage and
sadness
and
last words and
petty out of my system
so maybe the next book will
be contemplative
transcendent
rising above

just not feeling that
yet and not about
to fake it

damn it, Rob

"If you are filled with pride over how
free and intelligent and enlightened
you are in comparison to their
backward, antiquated ways, your
new knowledge has simply made you
arrogant. Watch your heart carefully,
because if you aren't more compassionate
and more kind and more understanding,
then you haven't grown at all."

—Rob Bell

operation: love us

loving your neighbor as yourself means
loving all the people you ever were

means loving my neighbor when she's
more like my 2007 self than my 2021 self

and yes this is way way easier to say
than actually do but let's keep trying

where's the pause button?

your faith shifts, you try to write about it
lay it all out from beginning to end

so people can see the what and the why
and be encouraged on their own journey

but the whole thing won't stop tipping,
shifting, moving, unraveling, crumbling for

FIVE DAMN SECONDS

so you can write something concrete

words are permanent and as someone who
has words out in the world in book form that

SHE DOES NOT BELIEVE ANYMORE

she is slightly sensitive about this

here she is writing a book about how she's
changing and growing and she can't even

stomach reading what she just wrote

she's not talking about cringing at the person she
was 10 years ago—she embraces that part of herself

she's talking about the person she was 10 *minutes* ago
the person who thinks a certain way and writes with

certain turns of phrase, from certain frames of mind
she's evolving faster than she can write and it's all

A WEE BIT DISCONCERTING

but nevertheless she aims to persist
because what other choice is there really?

yes I had to google it

Howard Thurman tells a story of a
famous teacher, who when urged to
consult a priest on his deathbed, said

no, I am curious to see what
happens in the next world
to me, who dies unshriven

oh my god new favorite word

the good ol' days

I'll admit sometimes I miss those days

knowing what I know now
I would never ever go back

but it wasn't a bad life, you know?

naive and blissfully unaware of how
toxic my faith was both to me and others

grateful for years left to heal

but more importantly to repair damage
I did to people around me because of

my white evangelical nationalistic
supremacist colonizing Christian beliefs

yes to all of dis

disaffected
dissatisfied
discontented
disbelieving
disenchanted
disentangled
disinterested
discombobulated
disillusioned
disgusted
dissociated
disconcerted
disheartened
dis sucks

we're separated

I'm stepping away from Christianity
while it gets its act together

I'd planned to get back together
but the more stuff that comes to light

the more it's looking like
we're headed toward divorce

fear is not invited

deconstruction feels scary
but the good news?

fear is actually the very thing
you're deconstructing

God says "God is love"
God says "do not fear"

and yet here we are

when we truly shed false beliefs
and believe God is actually love

our fear slowly fades away

hey there

speaking your truth
looks good on you

just wanted you to know

if I could turn back time

sometimes I sit in head-shaking bafflement
thinking of all the lies I accepted as truth

how on earth did I believe them for so long?
I found a partial answer in Proverbs 18:17

the first to present his case seems right until
another comes forward and questions him

when you're indoctrinated from the cradle
and told you hold the absolute only truth and

warned about "false arguments" you must
fervently oppose, come hell or high water

it all starts to make a lot more sense

preach, sister

"Anyone who gets to the end
of their life with the exact same
beliefs and opinions as they had
at the beginning is doing it wrong."

—**Sarah Bessey**

metanoia

a transliteration of the
Greek for turning around
resulting from penitence
or spiritual conversion

people want me to repent
before it's too late

they don't realize that's
what I've been doing

I'm repenting of beliefs
they still hold

take luck!

I see you over there
trying to
fix me
tsk tsk me
re-convert me
pray me back
into the fold

I wish you well
in your endeavors

God is love

I didn't leave evangelical christianity
because I balked at such high standards

I left because the dogmatic teaching
contradicted my deeply-held values

values I believe align with the
heart of God herself

underwhelmed

the more my faith shifted
the less interested I got in all

the tedious details of how I got
from point A to point B to point 172

because
who
even
really
cares

not me let's move on to
something actually interesting

for God so loved the (whole wide) world

I'm no longer interested in spending my entire life
picking apart the Bible and arguing it with people

when there are thousands of brilliant books out there
to read, explore, enjoy, learn from, and dialogue about

the Bible is one book from one place in one period of time
the world is teeming with peoples and cultures and eras

I want to climb out of the cardboard box and taste it all

amazingly enough, I do still have a thing for the Bible
in spite of all the people who wield it, literalize it, ruin it

I have smart/kind folks like Rob Bell, Pete Enns, Drew Hart,
RHE, Osheta Moore, and my brother Josh to thank for that

flowers for Libby

thank you Kay and Andy for / the space
to process deconstruction / faith shifting

with people I don't know / but already share
a bond with / what a gift and what makes it

even more powerful is how you've / shared it
during the hardest time in / your lives

I treasure your kindness and / will always
and forever / remember your sweet girl

a prayer for my ex

Mama God
have your way

unapologetic

I can be sassy
without being cruel

but I won't
give up the sass

it's who I am
if you don't like it

you don't like me
and that's fine

***you can't deconstruct forever*, they say**

at some point you need to construct again
you can't define yourself by anti- or ex- or not-

weird because that sums up my entire
lifetime as an evangelical Christian

a whole list of things/people I was against

I don't need to construct a new set of
theological beliefs because that's not how

I define myself these days / life is bigger than that
I define myself by me / and by love

on deconstructing and dismantling

deconstruction can't last forever / it's true
there's only so much to even deconstruct

but dismantling is a horse of a different color

as long as there are systems of oppression in place
I will devote my life to tearing them down

I will work to dismantle racism and white supremacy
misogyny and homophobia and the patriarchy and and and

these things won't crumble in my lifetime

I deconstructed so I could dismantle and I'm only
still talking about it so others can do it too

I never would have recognized oppressive systems
within Christianity without others opening my eyes

I didn't see how my erroneous beliefs about the Bible
contributed to—no, *created*—oppressive systems

deconstruction isn't the end—it's the path to dismantling

for b.

right before I put the final
touches on this book

you abruptly stopped trying
to convert me to your beliefs

asked if we could salvage
our relationship in some way

I said I'd give it a try
I feel a guarded hope

breathe

you really don't realize
how heavy a burden it is

to always have to be right
about your theological beliefs

until the weight is lifted
and you feel light as a leaf

gray is my love language

I thought everything was black and white
right or wrong, so good or so bad

this year I painted my bedroom gray
and bought myself gray bedding

I've loved gray for a lot of years now
and I've finally realized ,why

it's soothing, non-binary, calming
non-conforming, nuanced, mysterious

and as far as light wavelengths go, it's a mix of
every color and no colors, literally all-inclusive

that's a gray area used to seem threatening
and now I'm all *ooh, gray area! where? yay!*

write from your scars, they say

not your wounds and I mostly did
but I'll never be detached, unaffected

the journals filled with heartache collect
dust on my shelves because I vividly

remember and can't bring myself to look

as tempting as it sounds, my end goal
is not hardened armor no one can pierce

I want to stay open, vulnerable, be
someone who is softened by the pain

that arduous work will last a lifetime

b-r-a-v-e

I don't always feel brave
but I *am* brave

and sometimes I
am brave all alone

which is kind of extra brave

and I try not to
resent the people

who seem content to let me
always be the brave one

and their bravest act is to click "like"
on something brave *I* said

I want to tell you that
you can be brave too

I would love more
partners in crime

my herd

an ode to the women who
got me through this past year

my heart overflows with
love and gratitude

words fail me now but
a whole book is coming

I love you

cathartic

writing poems about my journey
has been so very therapeutic

so helpful so healing so freeing
I can't recommend it enough

unbelieve

if becoming a heretic
is what I have to do
to love people fully
and completely
it's a sacrifice
I'm willing to make

betting the farm

people people love love is my only mantra
if I'm doing it wrong, I'm cool with

getting to heaven, taking my chances
that Mama God knows my heart

tension

coming to terms with the fact that some
will find this book too much and others

not enough and they're right / hell, I
think both those things about it myself

depending on where you are on your journey
some poems are long behind you, some up ahead

some down a path you'll never take

I can't write custom personalized poems
for each of you as much as I'd love to

(just kidding, that sounds like a nightmare)

somebody take my laptop

how is this book
ever going to end
when I can't stop
writing poems?

resolved

well, Dad / I wrote a whole book
I hope this answers / everybody's questions

to their complete satisfaction / and puts
their hearts and minds / at ease

the one thing I'm not

lost means you don't know
where you are

or

how to get back to
where you came from

I know both of those things

I'm just not going back
and I don't know what lies ahead

but whatever I am
I'm not lost

star light star bright

"After so many years of trying to
cobble together a way of thinking
about God that makes sense so that I
can safely settle down with it, it all
turns to *nada*. There is no permanently
safe place to settle.

I will always be at sea, steering by the stars.

Yet as dark as this sounds, it provides
great relief, because it now sounds
truer than anything that came before."

—Barbara Brown Taylor

light at the end of the tunnel

I'm so much more at ease with uncertainty
now, more at peace with the unknown

I've fallen deeply in love with mystery

but I remember the intense discomfort
unnerving restlessness, the haunting fear

I filled journal after journal full of angst

it was so so so so so hard for
so many days and weeks and years

it really does get so much better, friend

but there's no way around it, over it, or
under it / you have to walk through it

and it helps if someone holds your hand

this right here

"Love, not answers."

—Madeleine L'Engle

where have I landed?

that's the thing, I can fly now
and damn what a glorious view

you can see so much from up here wow
and dang there are other birds too

I might descend, alight from time to time

but why would I land in any one place
for very long at all when I have wings

I've always always had wings

less / more

what I love / about poetry
is that the less / I say

the more room I leave / for you

Acknowledgments:

There's no way in hell I can thank all the people I need/want to thank who have loved and supported me on this journey, so I'm going to keep it short and sweet.

Thank you, Rachel Held Evans. (of course)

Thank you, all the authors I quoted in this book. I owe you so much.

Thank you, all the people ahead of me on the journey who had so much patience with me over the years.

Thank you, all of my friends and neighbors and acquaintances of other faiths who taught me so so much.

Thank you, Corrin, for always being my dear friend, my sounding board, and so so so much more.

Thank you, women in my private community, for helping me survive 2021.

Thank you, Kay and Andy, for the space to vent and process and be.

Thank you, Nya, Jenn, Becca, Amanda, Diane, Jennifer, Gloria, Ruth, Corrin, and Wendy for reading my book and offering really amazing helpful feedback.

Thank you, Mom and Dad, for raising me to have a kind, generous heart and to love and serve others.

Thank you, Josh and Jess, for your unconditional love and friendship and invigorating discussions.

Thank you, Steph and Daniel, for EVERYTHING. You literally (*literally*) saved my life this past year. I love being your neighbor.

Thank you, offspring, for walking this whole damn thing with me. I love you billions.

Thank you, Mama God/Jesus/whoever you are. I feel you with me.

Appendix A:

an apology to democrats (and Jesus)
August 4, 2011 (my blog)

Dear Democrats (and Jesus),

I don't know how else to do this but to just swallow my pride, jump in, and start saying I'm sorry for stuff. I think it would be a lot easier if I didn't have 35 years of judgmentalism and arrogance under my belt, but I guess it beats 65 or 75 years, right?

For the record, these aren't thoughts that just hit me this morning or anything. God's been working on my heart about this for a long time, but really in the past three years I'd say. And this past year most of all.

Am I stalling…? Here we go.

My Democrat friends, I'm sorry for assuming all this time that God was a Republican. I'm sorry for thinking that, if Jesus were walking the earth today he'd vote Republican hands-down, no questions asked.

I'm sorry for thinking that God mostly lives in America and that we are the center of the universe and that this is where you should be if you want to experience what it's like for God to bless a nation that does things right.

I'm sorry for being so narrowly focused on homosexuality and how wrong it is and abortion and how wrong it is, to the exclusion of many, many other issues. (The ones the Bible says over and over and over again that God actually cares about most.)

I'm sorry for mistaking my self-righteousness for righteousness. I'm sorry for labeling people who care about the poor and "social justice" as "liberal atheists" or worse. I'm sorry for blissfully ignoring the 2000+ verses in the Bible that talk about God's huge, huge, HUGE heart for the poor and oppressed and command me to be kind and merciful and giving and do all I can to bring them justice.

I'm sorry for saying that as long as I "have an eternal mindset," then it doesn't matter two hoots what I do to the beautiful earth God created. It's all going to be destroyed any minute anyway. Might as well live it up and waste, waste, waste!

I'm sorry for demanding that women not have abortions but then doing jack squat for them in their deepest hour of need.

I'm sorry for defending George W. Bush (and John McCain and Sarah Palin) no matter what they do or say, because as long as they're going to church on Sunday and believe Jesus is the way to heaven, then I know I'm on the right train, so get out of my way.

I'm sorry for thinking that sitting at my kitchen table and reading my Bible and praying for two hours makes me more holy than someone who is holding and rocking an orphan in Africa dying of AIDS.

I'm sorry for ever thinking that AIDS is a "gay people's problem."

I'm sorry for my condescending, plank-in-my-eye attitude when this whole time my gospel had a big, fat, humongous, gaping hole in it.

I'm sorry for thinking that "loving people" is code for "watering down the gospel" when, in fact, I'm the one who's been watering down the gospel this whole time.

I'm sorry for thinking that "getting people to heaven" is all that matters, and that their physical needs here on earth aren't that big a deal. I'm sorry for putting so much stock in someone praying a carefully-worded prayer that's not even in the Bible and ignoring the parts where it explains what it really means to be a follower of Jesus and surrendered to him.

I'm sorry for explaining away passages like Matthew 25:31-46 because I don't like the thought of God keeping me out of heaven just because I didn't help the poor.

I could go on for pages, so I'm putting the rest in a book.

Please know, my Democrat friends, that I'm not speaking for all Republicans. They aren't all as narrow-minded and mis-representative of the gospel as I've been. There are some wonderful, wonderful people out there who fly the elephant flag.

And please know, my Democrat friends, that I'm not jumping ship, switching parties, riding the donkey into town. In fact, I don't know that I want to align myself with a particular party ever again. I'm more concerned with God's politics these days than anything.

And I know now that many of you are too. It wasn't too terribly long ago that I seriously questioned how Democrats who called themselves Christians could sleep at night.

And last thing, my Democrat friends who don't share my faith. I apologize with all my heart for turning you off when it comes to Jesus. If you're offended by what he does/says in the Bible, that's one thing, and I can't do anything about that. But if you've been offended by me because I've been acting the exact opposite (prideful, Pharisaical, hypocritical) of how Jesus would act but calling myself his follower, then may I humbly ask your forgiveness?

I believe with everything in me that we are all sinners and that Jesus is our only hope for reconciliation to God and eternal life in heaven. I'm not throwing Jesus or God's Word out with the bathwater.

But the filthy, stinking bathwater has to go. I'm done clinging to a party line and slapping God's seal of approval on it without his permission. I pledge allegiance to my Savior. Period.

Forgive me?

Marla

Appendix B: Top 10 List of Garbage Books You Should Absolutely Read

#1: *Faith Unraveled* (Rachel Held Evans)
#2: *Out of Sorts* (Sarah Bessey)
#3: *The Bible Tells Me So* (Pete Enns)
#4: *What Is the Bible?* (Rob Bell)
#5 *The Dance of the Dissident Daughter* (Sue Monk Kidd)
#6: *The Very Good Gospel* (Lisa S. Harper)
#7: *Love Wins* (Rob Bell)
#8: *The Color of Compromise* (Jemar Tisby)
#9: *Native* (Kaitlin Curtice)
#10: *Dear White Peacemakers* (Osheta Moore)

Appendix C: The Intersection of Racism and Christianity

A few years ago, I committed the rest of my life to antiracism and eradicating white supremacy. This book touched only lightly on this topic, but I'm more passionate about it than anything else in my life.

In 2017, I began a lifelong journey to read and learn more from Black, Indigenous, and other People of Color. I'm sharing my journey on Instagram as @whitegirllearning. I invite you to join me.

I think it's immensely important for Christians to read widely, not just books about Christianity, but that's a good place to start.

In the words of Drew G. I. Hart, "Practically, I suggest that Christians from dominant culture change their reading habits so that those on the margins become the main stage."

Amen.

Here is a (**non-exhaustive**) list of books I've read that are written by BIPOC on the intersection of racism and the Christian faith.

Black authors
I'm Still Here (Austin Channing Brown)
The Very Good Gospel (Lisa Sharon Harper)
The Cross and the Lynching Tree (James H. Cone)
Trouble I've Seen (Drew G. I. Hart)
The Color of Compromise (Jemar Tisby)

Dear White Peacemakers (Osheta Moore)
Who Will Be a Witness? (Drew G. I. Hart)
I Bring the Voices of My People (Chanequa Walker-Barnes)
Be the Bridge (Latasha Morrison)
Reading While Black (Esau McCaulley)
My Soul Looks Back (James H. Cone)
Twelve Lies that Hold America Captive (Jonathan Walton)
Rethinking Incarceration (Dominique DuBois Gilliard)
How to Fight Racism (Jemar Tisby)
Just Mercy (Bryan Stevenson)

Indigenous authors
Native (Kaitlin Curtice)
Unsettling Truths (Mark Charles and Soong-Chan Rah)
The Four Vision Quests of Jesus (Steven Charleston)
Rescuing the Gospel from the Cowboys (Richard Twiss)
Custer Died for Your Sins (Vine Deloria, Jr.)
The Land Is Not Empty (Sarah Augustine)
God is Red (Vine Deloria, Jr.)

Asian authors
Rescuing Jesus (Deborah Jian Lee)
Raise Your Voice (Kathy Khang)
The Voices We Carry (J.S. Park)
Parenting Forward (Cindy Wang Brandt)
Prophetic Lament (Soong-Chan Rah)
Race & Place (David P. Leong)
Outside the Lines (Mihee Kim Kort)
Beyond Colorblind (Sarah Shin)

Latinx authors
Abuelita Faith (Kat Armas)
Mujerista Theology (Ada Maria Isasi Diaz)
The God Who Sees (Karen Gonzalez)
Seeing Jesus in East Harlem (Jose Humphreys)
Hermanas (Natalia Kohn, Noemi Vega Quiñones, Kristy Garza Robinson)

Multiple authors
Forgive Us (Mae Elise Cannon, Lisa Sharon Harper, Troy Jackson, Soong-Chan Rah)

Appendix D: More Books!!

Again, this is not an exhaustive list. I'll be reading books—and *writing* about books—for years and years to come.

Books That Changed My Mind About the Bible
Misreading Scripture With Western Eyes (E. Randolph Richards, Brandon J. O'Brien)
The Bible Tells Me So (Peter Enns)
What Is the Bible? (Rob Bell)
The Blue Parakeet (Scot McKnight)
Love Wins (Rob Bell)
The Sin of Certainty (Peter Enns)
The Very Good Gospel (Lisa Sharon Harper)
Inspired (Rachel Held Evans)
How the Bible Actually Works (Peter Enns)
The Christian Agnostic (Leslie D. Weatherhead)
The Cross and the Lynching Tree (James H. Cone)

Books that Opened My Eyes to the Oppression of Women
Dance of the Dissident Daughter (Sue Monk Kidd)
Jesus Feminist (Sarah Bessey)
A Year of Biblical Womanhood (Rachel Held Evans)
Half the Church (Carolyn Custis James)
Women Race & Class (Angela Y. Davis)
The Making of Biblical Womanhood (Beth Allison Barr)

Books that Opened My Eyes to the Truth of our "Christian" Nation
Stamped From the Beginning (Ibram X. Kendi)

Lies My Teacher Told Me (James Louwen)
An African American and Latinx History of the United States (Paul Ortiz)
An Indigenous People's History of the United States (Roxanne Dunbar-Ortiz)
The Making of Asian America (Erika Lee)
A Different Mirror (Ronald Takaki)
Between the World And Me (Ta-Nehisi Coates)
The Fire Next Time (James Baldwin)
No Name in the Street (James Baldwin)
The Color of Compromise (Jemar Tisby)
Unsettling Truths (Mark Charles and Soong-Chan Rah)
Jesus and John Wayne (Kristin Kobes Du Mez)
Stamped (Jason Reynolds, Ibram X. Kendi)
They Were Her Property (Stephanie E. Jones-Rogers)

Books That Made me LGBTQ+ Affirming
Blue Babies Pink (B.T. Harman)
Does Jesus Love Me? (Jeff Chu)
God & the Gay Christian (Matthew Vines)
Refocusing the Family (Amber Cantorna)
Changing Our Mind (David P. Gushee)
This Is How It Always Is (Laurie Frankel)
Outlove (Julie Rodgers)

Books that Resonated With Me on My Journey
Falling Free (Shannan Martin)
Irresistible Revolution (Shane Claiborne)
Interrupted (Jen Hatmaker)
7 (Jen Hatmaker)

Assimilate or Go Home (D.L. Mayfield)
Tattoos on the Heart (Gregory Boyle)
Leaving Church (Barbara Brown Taylor)
Walking on Water (Madeleine L'Engle)
Finding God in the Waves (Mike McHargue)
Falling Upward (Richard Rohr)
Bandersnatch (Erika Morrison)
The Very Worst Missionary (Jamie Wright)
Holy Envy (Barbara Brown Taylor)
Everything is Spiritual (Rob Bell)
Why I Believed (Kenneth W. Daniels)

Appendix E: Affirming Gay Marriage

Author B.T. Harman posted this powerful and thought-provoking list on Facebook in 2019 and graciously gave me permission to share the whole thing in this book.

Follow B.T. on Instagram: @bt_harman and read his compelling story at bluebabiespink.com.

19 Reasons Why Christians Are Moving Toward Affirming Gay Marriage

1. They know really kind gay people who love the Lord and are doing their best to honor him. They believe the many verses in the Bible that say a proof for real faith is loving your fellow believer. They see their gay friends doing this, bearing the Fruit of the Spirit, and believe their faith to be authentic.

2. They've studied the results of reparative therapy (the belief that people can change their orientation), and they understand that there is no scientific evidence that orientation can be changed. And they've listened to the Christian leaders of ex-gay ministries who've all said that orientation does not change through prayer, Bible reading, fasting, exorcism, etc.

3. Additionally, they may have talked to people who participated in reparative therapy years ago and heard their stories of pain and trauma.

4. They're aware of the fact that same-sex marriage is neither addressed nor condemned in the Bible.

5. These people recognize the psychological, emotional, and spiritual benefits of marriage and don't think it's healthy for 3-5% of the population to be excluded from that. They've looked at the data (and their own experience) that shows humans fare much better in marriage relationships.

6. They think that asking a gay person to stay single and alone for 80+ years is an incredibly heavy burden to bear. Yes, suffering is a part of the Christian faith, but they see how their LGBT friends have been crushed by this belief (suffering and crushing are very different things).

7. They've heard stories of (or spoken to) gay people who tried the single/celibate path, only to find that it increased their misery, sadness, anxiety, and depression. They do not believe that living in that state for a prolonged, unending, and debilitating period of time is the way of Jesus. They believe that the way of God, as revealed in Scripture, is one less of bone-crushing suffering and more of general thriving.

8. They realize that the church has over-emphasized the "gay issue" and married it with a political agenda. They see how this has devastated the mission of the Church in North America. They hate the fact that many non-believers instantly think "anti-gay" when they hear the word "Christian."

9. They don't believe that homosexuality is a sign of moral decay. They believe it is a mysterious, yet naturally occurring phenomenon that is present in 3-5% of the population (and present in hundreds of species of animals). They believe everyone is freaking out about it because it's a taboo topic. They likely believe wild sexual behavior is a sign of moral decay but straight folks sometimes exhibit that as well. But they don't think loving, monogamous gay couples and their children are a sign of moral decay.

10. They realize that, even if it's assumed that homosexuality is a sin, it's utterly harmless to non-gay people. Straight people, nor their children, are being recruited into a "gay lifestyle." They've talked to lots of gay people and believed them when they've said they did not choose to be gay. LGBT people aren't trying to increase their numbers and, therefore, aren't a threat to them or their churches.

11. They maybe know gay couples and their children, and they may see no difference between them and their straight counterparts. They see the health and the love, and, to them, that feels like a Jesus thing. They may believe God finds joy in these families.

12. They see thousands of verses in the Bible that Bible-believing Christians ignore on a daily basis. And they are often met with silence when they ask why they don't believe/practice those verses. They wonder why straight people are "allowed" to distance themselves from select verses, but gay people are not.

13. They realize that same-sex marriage poses no threat to straight marriages. They realize that, since SCOTUS approved gay marriage, not one straight marriage has been harmed by this ruling.

14. They believe the Bible, but they realize that writers in the Bronze Age or in 1st century Rome did not really have an understanding of homosexuality as we do today. Paul didn't have a car so he didn't give us driving tips. Similarly, we don't have any evidence that Paul knew any same-sex couples in a loving, monogamous relationship, and, therefore, wasn't writing to them when he spoke of what was likely a really nasty thing called pederasty.

15. They know the six anti-gay verses, but they believe that Scripture is to be interpreted in light of Scripture. Those verses must be put in context of the rest of the Bible and, ultimately, the character of God. Though we know Paul, the main contributor to the New Testament, sorta endorsed slavery, WE don't support slavery. We abhor slavery, because the Spirit has led us to an understanding that it is a morally repugnant practice. We worship God, not Scripture.

16. They don't believe that all gays are out to steal the rights of straight people. In fact, they realize that granting equal rights to gay people actually costs straight people nothing. It does them no harm.

17. They believe that supporting religious freedom AND gay rights is possible and noble. Just because some gays are suing

Christian cake bakers, they realize that there are millions of other LGBT folks who would not take this approach and who respect religious freedom. They see the nuance in the gay community and don't lump everyone into the same bucket of belief or ideology.

18. While they may believe it's best for kids to be raised by both a mother and a father, they understand that gay couples aren't stealing kids from straight homes. Gay couples are only acquiring kids the straight folks abandoned or making new ones through surrogates. They may believe that being pro-life means celebrating the birth of any child in any situation. They may believe that a child being raised with two loving same-sex parents is way better off than a homeless child being shuffled around the foster care system or being an unknown face in an orphanage.

19. They take a deep breath and rest easy at night knowing that this is not a make-or-break issue for the church. The church has weathered many bigger storms/controversies before this one. Gays will keep being gay. Straights will keep being straight. We'll all keep living, laughing, and working right alongside each other just like we have for thousands of years. There is no "culture war" (other than when the media incites us to hate each other). And Jesus and the Gospel will be just fine with or without our opinions on the topic.

Again, I can't speak for these folks, but just consider that maybe they have more reasons for their change of heart than "just giving in to the culture." Like you, maybe they came to their conclusions by sincere and prayerful means.

Appendix F: Where to Find the Quotes

reader beware (goodreads)
100% (*Plan B: Further Thoughts on Faith*, Anne Lamott)
precisely (Sarah Bessey quoting Rachel Held Evans in *Out of Sorts*, p. 66)
The Bible Tells Me So (*The Bible Tells Me So*, Peter Enns, p. 8)
escarpment of annihilation (*Faith Unraveled*, Rachel Held Evans, p. 22)
fortunately yes (*The Dance of the Dissident Daughter*, Sue Monk Kidd, p. 15)
me neither (*And It Was Good*, Madeleine L'Engle, p. 34)
yes and yes and yes (*The Dance of the Dissident Daughter*, Sue Monk Kidd, p. 147)
absolutely addled (*Work: A Story of Experience*, Louise May Alcott)
clapback (dictionary.com) (clapback lite: me)
can confirm (*Jesus Feminist*, Sarah Bessey, p. 15)
bulletproof vest / cable knit sweater (*Rising Strong*, Brené Brown, p. 52)
my favorite preacher (LIFE magazine Vol. 54, James Baldwin)
same (*7*, Jen Hatmaker, p. 23)
but I worked so hard on it (*Jesus Feminist*, Sarah Bessey, p. 16)
the age-old science/faith quandary (*The Bible Tells Me So*, Peter Enns, p. 69)
good point (*Finding God in the Waves*, Mike McHargue, p. 37)
you know about this, right? (*What Is the Bible?* Rob Bell, p. 117)
thank you, Rachel, once again (*Faith Unraveled*, Rachel Held Evans, p. 225)

Jesus Feminist (*Jesus Feminist,* Sarah Bessey, p. 13-14)

least favorite christian quote (Andy Stanley on Twitter)

on evangelicals as the "persecuted minority" (*Faith Unraveled,* Rachel Held Evans, p. 34)

the very good gospel (*The Very Good Gospel,* Lisa Sharon Harper, p. 13)

we have it backward (*Native,* Kaitlin Curtice, p. 25)

assimilate or go home (book by D.L. Mayfield)

our beautiful Muslim neighbors (*What Is the Bible?* Rob Bell, p. 149)

dear white peacemaker (*Dear White Peacemaker,* Osheta Moore, p. 256)

amen and amen (Robert Jones, Jr., @sonofbaldwin, on Twitter)

the color of compromise (book by Jemar Tisby)

more amens (*The Color of Compromise,* Jemar Tisby, p. 4)

say it louder (*Who Will Be a Witness?* Drew G. I. Hart, p. 107)

sad but the truest (*Faith Unraveled,* Rachel Held Evans, 117)

I saw this meme (eatliver.com)

once upon a time (*Love Wins,* Rob Bell, p. 110)

#goals (*Tattoos on the Heart,* Gregory Boyle, p. 192)

god and the gay christian (book by Matthew Vines)

Jesus and John Wayne (book by Kristin Kobes Du Mez)

the realest thing (*Learning to Walk in the Dark,* Barbara Brown Taylor, p. 140)

mine fit in a coin purse (*Learning to Walk in the Dark,* Barbara Brown Taylor, p. 138)

the whole spectrum (*Jesus Feminist,* Sarah Bessey, p. 56)

he ain't kidding (*What Is the Bible?* Rob Bell, p. 319)

damn it, Rob (*What Is the Bible?* Rob Bell, p. 321)

yes I had to google it (*Meditations of the Heart,* Howard Thurman, p. 141)

if I could turn back time (*Why I Believed*, Kenneth W. Daniels, p. 86)

preach, sister (*Out of Sorts,* Sarah Bessey, p. 88)

star light star bright (*Learning to Walk in the Dark,* Barbara Brown Taylor, p. 140)

this right here (*Walking on Water,* Madeleine L'Engle, p. 108)

Appendix G: Other Books I've Written

I can't, in good conscience, recommend most of my old books, but here they are if you want to see who I was and how I've grown. (I'm working up the courage to reread some of them myself.)

From Blushing Bride to Wedded Wife (Harvest House, 2006)
I wrote this book with six whopping years of marriage under my belt. The theology is terrible, but the writing is really good (and funny). It would be funnier if I were still married.

Is That All He Thinks About? (Harvest House, 2007)
Yes, I wrote a whole book on sex from a conservative Christian point of view. I knew nothing. And yet I filled an entire book. It's also well-written and funny. (please don't read it)

Changing the World One Diaper at a Time (Harvest House, 2008)
It's been a decade since I read this one, but I imagine it would be less triggering than the first two. My marriage didn't last, but my kids (20, 19, and 15) have turned out great so far.

Expecting (Howard Books, 2009)
This is the only one of my traditionally-published books that's still in print (thank goodness). It's a "devotional" full of prayers that would most likely make me cringe. I won't be rereading it.

Self-Published Ebooks:

The Husband's Guide to Getting Lucky (2011)

This is the book I said I'd never write. But I got a whole lot of emails from guys asking for their own version of *Is That All He Thinks About?* It's a funny book (and probably very problematic). Also, my husband had a massive heart attack four months after I wrote it, so um.

Once Upon the Internet (2012)

In 2008-2009, our family of five (our daughters were 7, 6, and 2) went to 52 Zoos in 52 Weeks. We stayed with 33 families, 17 of them we'd only ever met on the internet. People thought we were big ol' weirdos. We were. But, god, what a lot of great memories.

The Wife Life (2013)

When my first book, *Blushing Bride*, went out of print, there wasn't an ebook version of it available to keep it alive. So I literally typed up the whole entire thing, made edits (because I had changed my mind quite a bit in seven years), added some funny, and there you go.

We Dream of Cambodia (2014)

My husband and I took a missions trip to Cambodia in 2010. We promised our girls we'd take them on the next one. In December 2011, we spent 5 weeks in Cambodia as a family, made plans to move there, then our entire lives got derailed. This book tells that story.

An Unschooling Manifesto (2014)

Instead of moving to Cambodia, we piled up medical debt, lost our house, and I decided to homeschool our kids for fun.

Homeschooling quickly morphed into unschooling, and this is my bold statement about why I thought our unconventional decision was right for us at the time.

The Storm (2015)
My husband's heart attack was followed by six weeks of normalcy, five weeks in Cambodia, two more weeks of normalcy, then three years of anxiety, depression, and panic attacks. It changed him—and us—forever. I wouldn't know the extent of it until five years after I wrote the book.

Shipwrecked (2017)
After we lost our house, we moved into a 787-square foot apartment in a complex that housed primarily refugees. It turned out to be one of the most magical (and also very difficult) years of our lives. We made friends; our neighbors fed and loved us; and our lives were changed.

What Makes You Fart? (2017)
I don't know about you, but when I'm in my "happy place," I fart. For me, that's bookstores. 10 out of 10 times. Scientifically speaking, your body releases gas when you're relaxed and all is working smoothly. To find out your life's passion, just figure out what makes you fart.

Unschooling: The Honest Truth (2018)
If you're looking for a book about how to unschool, you should read *An Unschooling Manifesto*, not this one. This one is very angsty and talks about how hard our lives were in Cambodia (and

I didn't know the half of it). It's a good read for parents of teenagers looking for solidarity.

Made in the USA
Monee, IL
01 September 2022